DRAW YOUR OWN FONTS

30 alphabets to scribble, sketch and make your own

Tony Seddon

DRAW YOUR OWN FONTS

30 alphabets to scribble, sketch and make your own

Ivy Press

First published in the UK in 2013 by
Ivy Press
210 High Street
Lewes
East Sussex BN7 2NS, UK
www.ivypress.co.uk

British Library Cataloguing-in-Publication Data

A catalogue record for this book is available from
the British Library

ISBN: 978-1-908005-81-6

This book was conceived, designed & produced by
Ivy Press

Creative Director: Peter Bridgewater
Publisher: Susan Kelly
Commissioning Editor: Sophie Collins
Art Director: Wayne Blades
Senior Editor: Jayne Ansell
Designer: Tony Seddon

Printed in China
Colour Origination by Ivy Press Reprographics

Distributed worldwide (except North America)
by Thames & Hudson Ltd., 181A High Holborn,
London WC1V 7QX, United Kingdom

10 9 8 7 6 5 4 3 2 1

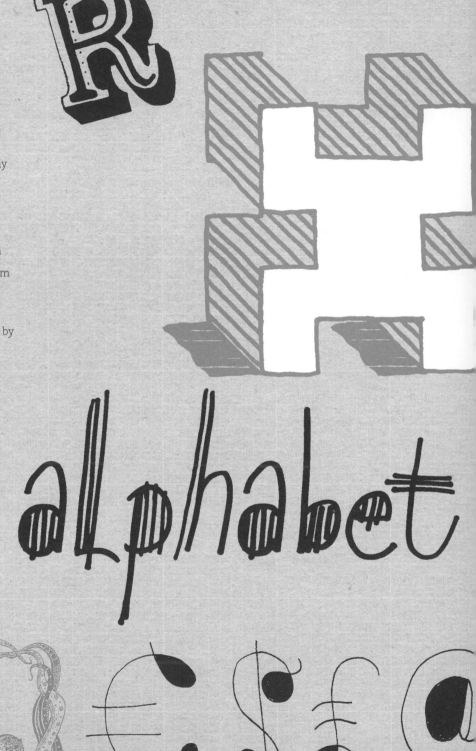

CONTENTS

About Hand Lettering	6
Developing a Skill Set	7
Tracing & Tampering	8
Understanding Letterforms	9

THE ALPHABETS — 11

HOW TO USE YOUR FONTS — 143

How Computers Handle Fonts	144
Bitmap Versus Vector	146
Drawing & Scanning Fonts	148
Drawing with Vectors	150
Digitizing Your Fonts	152

The Anatomy of a Font	156
Glossary	157
About the Font Designers	159
Acknowledgements	160

ABOUT HAND LETTERING

Once upon a time there was nothing but hand lettering, and this kept a lot of monks in gainful employment whilst they weren't otherwise occupied with praying and brewing. This was all well and good, but it did mean that books took absolutely ages to put together, and that the range of subjects covered was pretty limited (unless you were really into religion, of course).

It also meant that books were enormously expensive. So expensive, in fact, that hardly anyone could afford them. So for centuries few people learned to read, and even if they could there was no point because they couldn't buy anything to read anyway. As for the gig flyer market, it was a total non-starter back in those days.

All this began to change in the first half of the 15th century, when folk such as Johannes Gutenberg, Nicolas Jenson and William Caxton realized that there was money to be made in printing books and posters on a much larger scale – and in a lot less time than the guys up at the monastery could manage. In fact, it was Caxton who kick-started the burgeoning flyer scene when he printed some to advertise his own shop – smart fellow. Literacy levels quickly began to grow and something called the 'publishing industry' was invented.

Fast forward through movable wood and metal type, the mechanization of typesetting via Linotype and Monotype hot metal machines, Letraset – *a form of rub-down lettering that arrived on a plastic sheet* – and photo typesetting, and we arrive at 1984 and the first Apple Macintosh. This changed everything. Since then designers and non-designers alike have gradually been handed total typographic control and can make pretty much any letter shapes they want to, limited only by their own creativity and eye for detail.

However, for some time a groundswell of opinion has grown around the fact that anyone can buy a Mac – *or a PC, let's not be partisan* – and create type. Mutterings of lost skills and generic design solutions have become rife. This has seen a resurgence in the art of hand lettering, along with a whole host of other design- and craft-related skills. We are presently living in a new era of popularity for the 'handmade', with no sign of its relevance waning as other faddish movements have during recent decades.

But what else is there to recommend hand lettering? Well, there's one massively important point to make. Anyone can select a typeface, change the point size, and add some colour. With the style set, the type will be uniform and consistent. However, if you take the same piece of text and hand letter it, it's unique. Hand letter it again next week, and again it'll be equally unique. *That's what's so great about hand lettering — it's totally yours,* and creatively speaking it will always belong to you. Keep reading and you'll see what I mean.

DEVELOPING A SKILL SET

If you're a seasoned designer, there's a good chance that you'll have an extensive knowledge of type. Type underpins every area of graphic design because type + image = information, and that's what we're all about. If you're at the start of your creative career, or if you're a part-time lover of type, you may need a bit more help to get started on the path to hand-lettering success.

When I began my career as a graphic designer towards the end of the 1980s, the manuscript for a book was turned into type by a typesetter. The 'galleys' (or pages) of type arrived on a long roll of paper that you carved up with an X-Acto knife or scalpel and stuck to a board with either hot wax or this amazing stuff called 'Cow Gum' (which could also be used to make serviceable squash balls).

This meant that we had to learn how to hand-render type in order to create initial client visuals, and one of my first assignments at art college involved hand lettering a phrase in a randomly allocated typeface. I was given a specimen sheet of a typeface called Walbaum 374 and proceeded to hand letter the phrase *Et in Arcadia Ego* (in purple gouache on stretched cartridge paper, which looked good at the time). It was my first proper hand-lettering experience. If I'd been asked to hand letter the words the way I wanted I would have produced who-knows-what, but because I was required to replicate an existing typeface as accurately as possible I learned something about type.

It was a good way to start, and I recommend that you try something similar in order to get used to drawing standard letterforms. You don't need specimen sheets, of course; in fact it's easier to work from a piece of type that you've seen and liked. Be sure to start with a typeface that isn't itself hand-drawn as that would defeat the object of this exercise. *Work with a pencil to begin with (so you can erase the inevitable early slip-ups)* and try to render what you see as precisely as possible, looking closely at the shapes and proportions of each letter-form and the contrast in the width of the strokes. It'll be tempting to simply trace over the original, but resist the urge to do this in the first instance as you'll gain nothing by doing that. Almost anyone with a steady hand can trace a piece of type.

Don't go into this expecting your initial efforts to look amazing as it takes practice, but hopefully in time you'll find that you can reproduce a pretty good version of Bodoni or Benton, Garamond or Gill Sans. What you're aiming for is effectively a slightly less than perfect version of the original type sample. Once you feel confident that you can do this, it's time to raise the bar a little higher.

TRACING & TAMPERING

• •

Hopefully you've followed the advice about getting to grips with drawing regular letterforms (slapped wrist if not), as guess what, I'm about to lift the embargo on tracing. I don't want to encourage you to copy entire letterforms directly, of course, but rather to use tracing as a means of creating new and therefore unique examples.

The scenario is that you've got an idea in your head for a project and you want to incorporate some handmade elements. You know the space the type needs to fit into, what size the type should be, what the line breaks are and so on, but you can't simply typeset it as you really want it to be hand-drawn. One way to approach this is to select a typeface that's similar in proportion or style – maybe a script or an italic serif or whatever – and use it to roughly create the typographic arrangement that you need for your piece. Once you have that, run it through your printer at the size you want to use it and trace it in pencil to provide the skeleton for your own hand-drawn typography. If you use a blue pencil, the sketch work won't pick up on a scanner – *we talk about this in more detail on pages 148–149.*

Now you can have all kinds of lettering fun by tampering with each of the letterforms. Call it 'font customizing' if you like. The aim is to build on the basic letterforms by either adding or subtracting detail until you achieve the look you're after. You can extend serifs, add flourishes, exaggerate stroke contrasts, or completely deconstruct the original letterforms. The only limits with hand-drawn typefaces are those

imposed by either you, the project, or your client (if you have one). However, remember always to keep an eye on readability as it's all too easy to get carried away with embellishing and forget that someone might actually have to decipher what the text says. When you're happy with the results, go over the sketched guides with black ink to create your final line work.

This method is particularly suitable for hand drawing complete words or collections of words used to form a headline or phrase, but you can use it just as effectively for creating individual characters that are going to form a complete character set. If you are working on a full alphabet, ensure you work at a consistent size when tracing and customizing each character – it's a nightmare to try and rationalize everything at the end of the process if you don't.

With enough practice, you'll eventually be able to dispense with tracing altogether when creating your own hand-drawn typefaces and digital fonts. That doesn't mean you have to turn your back on tracing altogether, of course, as many a creative project is built on the foundations of another. Leave it in your toolbox of typographic tricks until the next time you need some extra help.

UNDERSTANDING LETTERFORMS

There's an argument, undeniably valid, that if you're hand drawing typefaces then a knowledge of regular letterforms isn't really necessary. And that's fair enough, I suppose. However, I would counter that argument by saying it applies only when creating a specific style of hand lettering, the kind that's not based on any of the traditional typefaces.

If you're looking to make a character set of overtly abstract letterforms then no problem, it's fine to throw everything out of the window and head in whichever direction you feel. But for me, it's important to understand how letterforms work. The anatomy of type is important, as a little knowledge will allow you to talk the talk with your colleagues *(or your dog, if you work on your own like me)* about the various elements and characteristics of a letterform. The illustration on page 156 will help you get to grips with the correct terminology.

It's just as important to consider observing consistent standards such as x- and cap-heights when you're creating a full character set for hand-drawn typefaces as it is for regular digital fonts. It's not compulsory, of course, as some fonts are bound to require a more free-form quality, but here's a bit of friendly advice from someone who learned the hard way. If you fail to give the basic structure of your letterforms any thought, your efforts are in danger of looking amateurish and ill-considered, a bit like a high-school project compared with a professional commission. Even though hand-drawn faces represent the free form, they should still be structured and consistent if they're going to work well.

If you feel that you could use some help with understanding how letterforms work, try this simple exercise. Choose a handful of regular typefaces that you either like or think would look good together, then pick a couple of the lower case characters from each. The lowercase 'a' and 'g' are good choices because they contain a lot of the features found in the majority of characters, such as bowls, tails, counters, links and loops (see the illustration on page 156 if these don't mean anything). Using whatever software you have to hand, position the characters on a computer screen in an aligned stack to see how the x-heights, ascenders or descenders, bowls, counter shapes or serifs compare. Better still, grab some tracing paper and trace each character, overlaying each one, to really see how they differ. It's a surprisingly enlightening experience which I highly recommend, and it's the best way to get to grips with the way the internal and external shapes of individual characters are formed.

(see page 156 for the Anatomy of a Font)

@ALFAB

mnopq

ALPHA

SHEET123

Q ABC

ETOS

123 M

BET1 ∞

!?@$&%£ THE

ALPHABETS

BUTTERMAN

This font conjures up images of a comedy super hero – a strong but slightly rotund character whose adventures bring success and disaster in equal measure. Designer Scott Suttey had this hero – 'The Butter Man' – in mind when he created this font, picturing his suit with its trademark logo emblazoned across the front.

ANATOMY OF THE FONT

Each glyph from the character set of Butterman appears to be cut from a single block. Character widths are proportional to allow for conventionally spaced lettering, and round glyphs are based on perfect circles.

KEY FONT DETAILS

• None of the glyphs feature counters or eyes
• Some lower case glyphs such as the 's' echo the upper case forms, whilst others contain slightly more detail

NATURAL PARTNERS

• The chunky 3D characters of this font need a strong partner, so try a solid geometric sans serif such as **Klavika** or **Scala Sans**.

FONT FEATURES

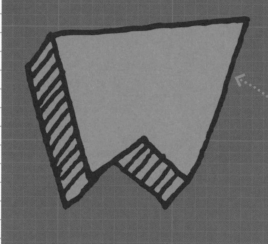

● All glyphs are solid blocks

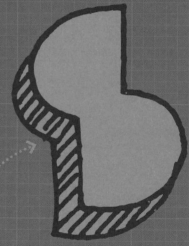

● The 'S' is constructed from a pair of semi-circles

BUTTERMAN

ABCDEFGHIJ
KLMNOPQRS
TUVWXYZ
À Ç É Ë Ï Ñ Õ Ô Ü ß
1 2 3 4 5 6 7 8 9 0

BUTTERMAN

a b c d e f g h i j

k l m n o p q r s

t u v w x y z

(à ç é ï ñ ô ü ß)

? ! @ $ & % £ £ ; ; : .

DRAW YOUR OWN

ABCDEFG
HIJKLMN
OPQRST
UVWXYZ
FAITH

CUPID

Heavy block typefaces are not always synonymous with delicacy, but illustrator Tonwen Jones wanted to create a font that baulked that trend. Curiously, the disproportionately tiny wings and passing clouds provide the font with an angelic quality that would otherwise be absent.

ANATOMY OF THE FONT

A variable alignment to the baseline helps to give this font the impression that it's hovering in the air. The wing-like embellishments vary in size and position from glyph to glyph, creating a charming sense of animated movement.

KEY FONT DETAILS

• Counters are rounded for some glyphs (D, O, P, and Q) and squared for others (A, B, and R)

• Cloud embellishments mean letter spacing must be kept very loose

NATURAL PARTNERS

• This is a one-off font, but many sans serif text fonts such as **Univers** could partner it well. You could also try a slab serif such as **Rockwell** (look at the upper case **I**).

FONT FEATURES

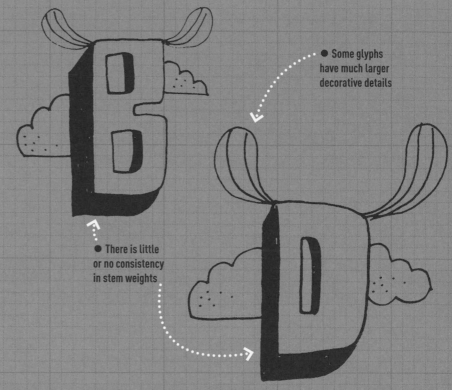

• Some glyphs have much larger decorative details

• There is little or no consistency in stem weights

A B C D E F
G H I J K L
M N O P Q R
S T U V W
X Y Z

CUPID

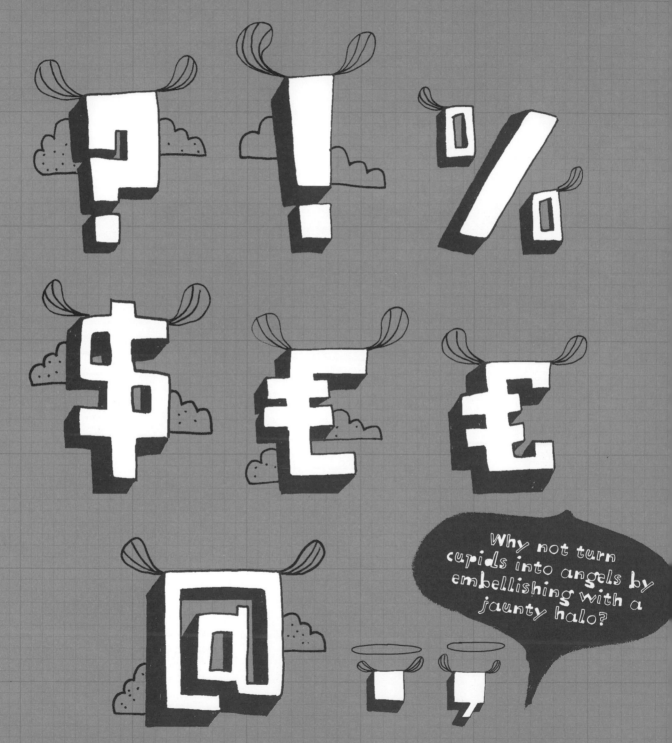

DRAW YOUR OWN

STEADMAN

Design solutions can often result from 'happy accidents'. Dave Pentland was developing a handwritten-style font, but discovered that the original drawings looked better reversed out after scanning and outlining. The font is named after Dave's favourite illustrator, Ralph Steadman.

ANATOMY OF THE FONT

The majority of glyphs in this typeface feature additional line work running parallel to the stems, enhancing the 'sketched' look associated with Ralph Steadman. A double line at the end of the stems and cross strokes form serifs.

KEY FONT DETAILS

• Counters are completely solid, meaning some glyphs appear to be much bolder
• The tail of the 'Q' is formed from the same double line style as the serifs
• Lower case 'a' has no serifs

NATURAL PARTNERS

• A neat serif font such as New Baskerville or Bell will work well with this freeform font with its own small serif details.

FONT FEATURES

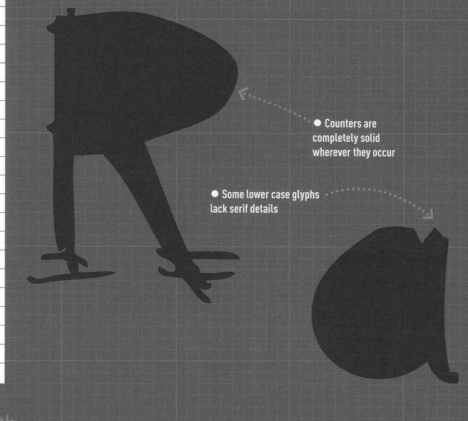

● Counters are completely solid wherever they occur

● Some lower case glyphs lack serif details

ABCDEF
GHIJKLM
NOPQRS
TUVWXY
Z.?!@£":$()

STEADMAN

a b c d e f
g h i j k l m
n o p q r s
t u v w x y z
ñ ü ß é à ô ï ç

DRAW YOUR OWN

SCIENCE LESSON

A desire to own a molecular modelling kit of the kind found in school science labs, and the acquisition of one in a second-hand store, inspired designer Wayne Blades to design this high-tech font. Needless to say, the molecular models never got made. The drop shadows were added in Photoshop post-scanning.

ANATOMY OF THE FONT

One of the more detailed fonts in this book, Science Lesson actually uses just a few basic elements to construct the relatively complex letterforms. The letters use a repeat 'molecule' to join each stroke formed by hand-drawn rules. At first glance the font appears to be monospaced, but it is in fact proportional.

KEY FONT DETAILS

• The 'B' is formed from diagonal, vertical and horizontal strokes to avoid potential misidentification as an '8', which is formed from diagonal strokes only
• The 'Q' is the only glyph with strokes that cross without a linking molecule element

NATURAL PARTNERS

• The scientific theme of this illustrative font should be carried through to accompanying text using fonts such as DIN or Neotech.

FONT FEATURES

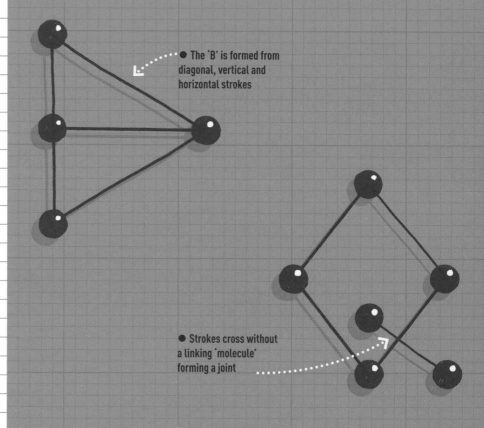

• The 'B' is formed from diagonal, vertical and horizontal strokes

• Strokes cross without a linking 'molecule' forming a joint

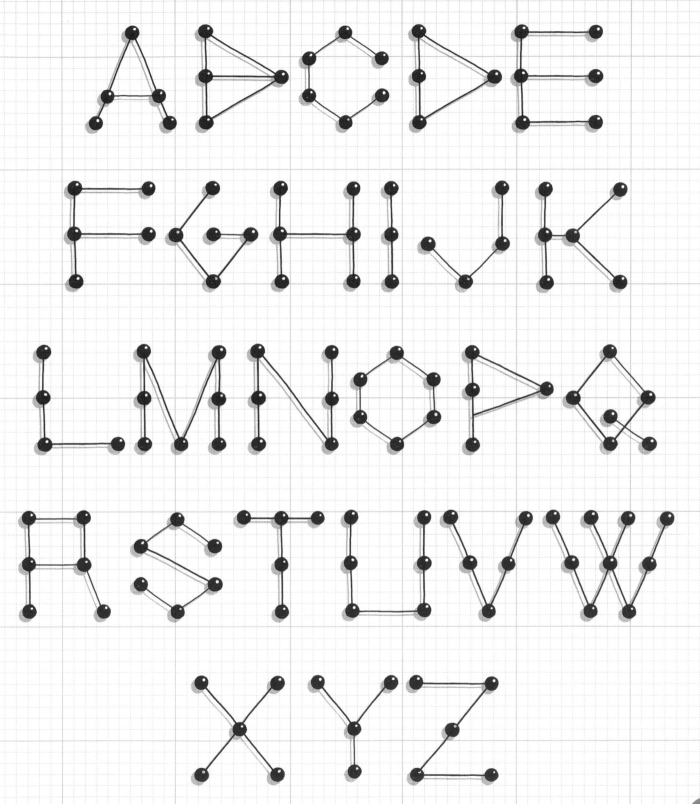

CONTROL CHAOS

Sarah Lu's font has been around since 1999 – it's scrawled in various forms over the many sketchbooks that record her thoughts, graphic ideas, loves and hates. The basic letterforms shown here are perfect for adding cross-hatching, drop shadows, or overlay patterns.

ANATOMY OF THE FONT

A more conventional typeface than some of the others featured in this book, Control Chaos features proportional character widths with glyphs more-or-less aligned to a consistent baseline. Tight spacing of this relatively condensed font makes it useful for headlines, or comic book speech bubbles.

KEY FONT DETAILS

• The leg of the 'R' terminates slightly above the baseline

• The lower bowl of the 'S' is much larger than the upper bowl

NATURAL PARTNERS

• Don't be tempted to pair any typeface with a 'cartoon' look to this font. Try bolder sans serifs such as **Franklin Gothic** or **Lucida Sans**.

FONT FEATURES

R S

• The lower bowl of the 'S' is proportionally much larger

• The leg of the 'R' terminates above the baseline

CONTROL CHAOS

ABCDEFGHI
JKLMNOPQ
RSTUVWXYZ
1234567890

abcdefghi
jklmnopqr
stuvwxyz
@£()?!&
)(/.,"%

DRAW YOUR OWN

ORIGAMI

When asked to develop a typeface for use on an Eastern-influenced retailer's website, illustrator Sarah Lu produced this carefully folded font. Based loosely on the font Alako Bold without echoing exact character shapes, the three-dimensional characters can actually be constructed from strips of paper.

ANATOMY OF THE FONT

Undoubtedly a novelty font with very specific potential usage, Origami's structure closely follows paper-folding rules. Shading on the areas of each glyph that are 'behind' others enhance the 3D qualities of the font.

KEY FONT DETAILS

• The cross strokes are double thickness in order to stay true to the limitations of real origami

• All glyphs are lower case

NATURAL PARTNERS

• Origami by its very nature is highly structured, so a structured sans serif will partner it well. Take a look at Eurostile, or perhaps Jeunesse Sans if you want to combine Origami with running text.

FONT FEATURES

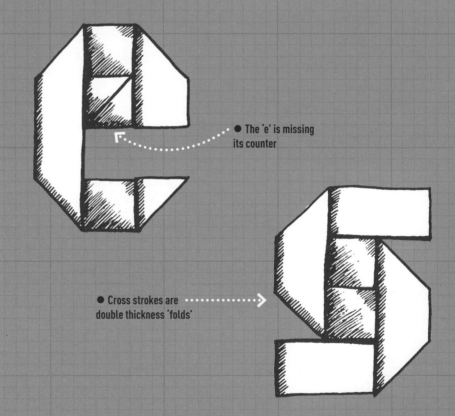

The 'e' is missing its counter

Cross strokes are double thickness 'folds'

abcdefghij
klmnopqrs
tuvwxyz
1234567 8
90".;:"?()!

ORIGAMI

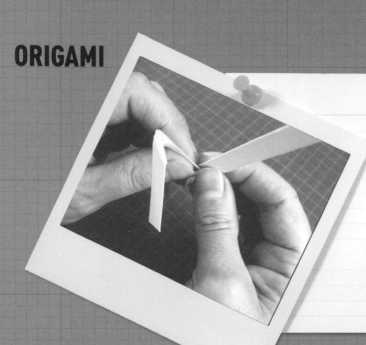

Start with strips of paper...

Fold, fold and fold again... and maybe fold a few times more, depending on which letter you're creating...

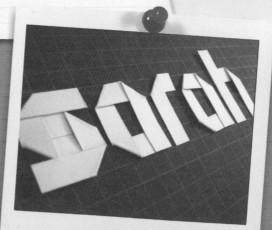

DRAW YOUR OWN

KNIT

We're not sure if it's actually possible to knit this font for real, but it would make for an interesting challenge for anyone who, like its designer Vanessa Hamilton, knows their box stitch from their ribbing stitch. Personally, I'd rather draw it than knit it. This is one of the more geometric fonts in the book.

ANATOMY OF THE FONT

Another out-and-out novelty font, Knit is surprisingly legible, given the high level of decorative detailing used in the design. This is largely due to the highly geometric character shapes which fit to a regular grid.

KEY FONT DETAILS

• The cross strokes vary in width in order to incorporate the necessary features of the more detailed glyphs
• The bowls are stepped rather than curved

NATURAL PARTNERS

• Geometric fonts such as **Franklin Gothic** or **Futura** will certainly make suitable partners for this unusual take on font design, but it's such a one-off that almost any geometric sans serif could work.

FONT FEATURES

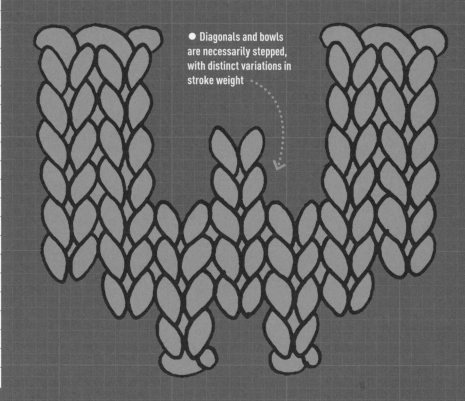

● Diagonals and bowls are necessarily stepped, with distinct variations in stroke weight

ABCDEF
GHIJKL
MNOPQ
RSTUV
WXYZ

KNIT

0123456789

NÜMĔRÏ

&?!0£$

[."]

DRAW YOUR OWN

FILL IN

We mentioned earlier that fonts can be derived from the designer's handwriting, and this is another good example. Emma Frith uses this style for writing signs and labels, and it was ostensibly created idly while 101 other important tasks were on her mind. Will she ever be able to absently draw it again now?

ANATOMY OF THE FONT

This is essentially a handwriting font so isn't structured with any regular proportion, consistent cap height or base alignment. It's precisely these qualities that help to make handwriting fonts look authentic.

KEY FONT DETAILS

• The 'B' and 'D' are the only glyphs that are completely filled in

• The elongated leg of the 'R' ensures its cap height is noticeably taller than any other character in the set

NATURAL PARTNERS

• It's possible to partner a handwriting font with just about anything as long as it's not another handwriting font. Try a classic sans serif however, something like Century Gothic or Helvetica Neue.

FONT FEATURES

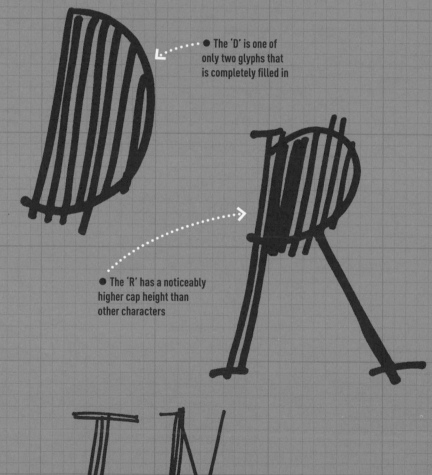

• The 'D' is one of only two glyphs that is completely filled in

• The 'R' has a noticeably higher cap height than other characters

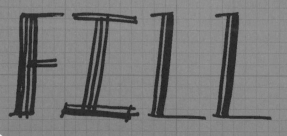

ABCDEFGHI
JKLMNOP
QRSTUVW
XYZ 123
4567890

abcdefghij
klmnopq
rstuvwxyz
?!¿!%$£&@""
,,()

DRAW YOUR OWN

SKINNY FRINGE

Take a look at some examples of Victorian poster design, and you'll realize where Michelle Tilly's inspiration for this font originated. Like the illustration style of the day, hand-carved wood type often used hatched lines to create tints and drop shadows before the invention of modern printing techniques.

ANATOMY OF THE FONT
Essentially a condensed display face, Skinny Fringe is a highly legible font with slightly unusual proportions. The 'M' and 'N' occupy the same character width yet the 'A' is much wider than both, adding to the quirkiness of this flexible font.

KEY FONT DETAILS
• The upper half of the 'S' overhangs the lower half and displays a forward-leaning angle of stress compared with other glyphs, which are more upright

NATURAL PARTNERS
• The Victorian influences behind this font give a clear indication that other faces with similar origins of style will make good choices. Try **Clarendon** or **Grotesque** to retain the retro feel.

FONT FEATURES

● Font is fairly condensed, as evidenced by the character width of the 'M'

● The 'S' displays a different angle of stress to other characters

SKINNY FRINGE

A B C D E F

G H I J K L

M N O P Q R

S T U V W X

Y Z

SKINNY FRINGE

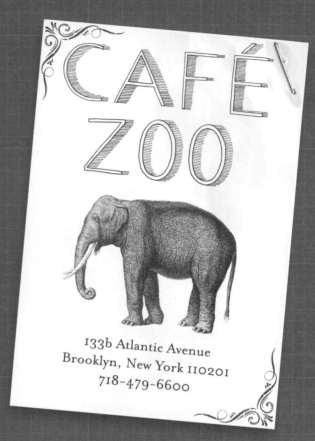

CAFÉ ZOO

133b Atlantic Avenue
Brooklyn, New York 110201
718-479-6600

DRAW YOUR OWN

BUILDINGS

As a child Tonwen Jones wanted to see her name spelt out in buildings, but when her plan to become a millionaire failed, she drew this typeface instead. It's not quite the same thing, but she'll make do with her alphabet metropolis until that inevitable lottery win... Any day now...

ANATOMY OF THE FONT

A curious font that is clearly not designed for maximum ease of readability, Buildings is really all about having some fun with a typeface. Try 'lighting' some of the windows to create a night-time effect.

KEY FONT DETAILS

• The actual character shapes are the least visible feature of the design
• Bowls, counters and eyes are all squared

NATURAL PARTNERS

• As this font is so highly illustrative the perfect pairing is hard to pin down, so why not carry on the fun and go for something like **Broadway**. If you want to set some running text, give Ehrhardt a try.

FONT FEATURES

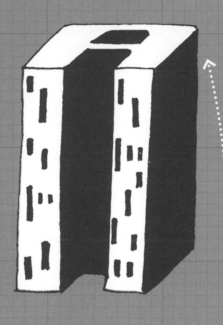

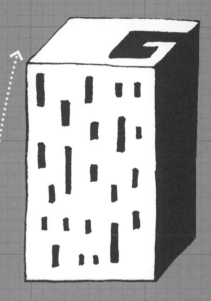

● Stroke width varies considerably between characters

BUILDINGS

Bring your alphabet metropolis to life by decorating with a city-scape backdrop.

DRAW YOUR OWN

FTI-64

Designer Lee Suttey likes to sketch when he's trying to form ideas for graphic design commissions. He also likes to sketch when he's trying to avoid working. This font is composed of characters selected from his collection of doodled glyphs and is perfect for projects where the pen must be mightier than the mouse.

ANATOMY OF THE FONT

FTI-64 has a great illustrative feel to it because of the retention of the pencil shading on the 3D characters. The font can be used comfortably for a wide range of applications.

KEY FONT DETAILS

• Diagonal strokes and stems vary in width and are slightly curved
• Some glyphs curve inwards at the baseline

NATURAL PARTNERS

• A sans serif or slab serif would partner this font well as a choice for accompanying text. Try **Dax**, which has similar qualities to the basic forms of FTI-64, or perhaps Glypha, which is a characterful slab.

FONT FEATURES

● Stem protrudes slightly beyond the cap height on some glyphs

● Strokes are often curved with an inward movement at the baseline

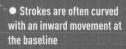

ABCDEFGHIJK
LMNOPQRS
TUVWXYZ
ÑÜBÉÅÔÏÇ
1234567890

abcdefghijk
lmnopqrs
tuvwxyz?!
(ñüßéàôïç)
@$&%£"":.

DRAW YOUR OWN

SLIME

Toy slime is a lot of fun to play with, and when our designer bought some for her young nephew she hid plastic insects in it and told him the slime had eyes. Very sweet but slightly scary at the same time! The idea stuck and next birthday, this font was designed for his card.

FONT FEATURES

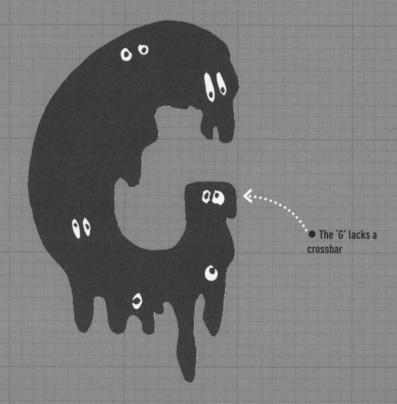

The 'G' lacks a crossbar

ANATOMY OF THE FONT

A classically spooky take on the novelty Halloween font, or simply a great bit of fun for children with a vivid imagination. Slime works well in any situation where an injection of humour is required for a project that doesn't take itself too seriously.

KEY FONT DETAILS

• There's no crossbar on the 'G'
• The loop of the lower case 'g' sits on the baseline instead of below it

NATURAL PARTNERS

• As with most highly illustrative fonts, it's difficult to pick fonts that pair naturally with it. Again, a sans serif font is likely to work best due to its plain letterforms. Good old Helvetica is a fair choice.

SLIME

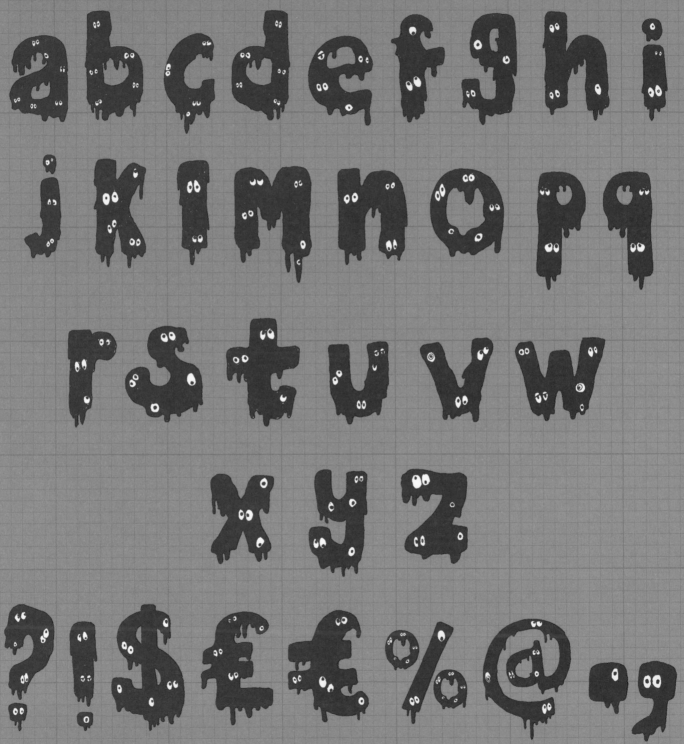

DRAW YOUR OWN

DEEP CAPITALS

This font is easy-to-read, even from a distance, and has that distinctive handmade quirkiness inherent in Tonwen Jones' illustration style. Combinations of upper- and lower-case characters provide mixed cap and x-heights without affecting legibility, creating a dynamic look for headline styling.

ANATOMY OF THE FONT

The erratic cap and x-heights of this font provide a lively and uneven feel for the character set but the face is still highly legible, even at small sizes which is unusual for a hand-drawn font. Character heights and therefore widths can be adjusted even further in order to fit text to a particular measure.

KEY FONT DETAILS

• Counters are filled in to give a slightly heftier feel to some characters

• The cap 'S' doesn't follow any rules set by other glyphs, lacking flat sides and an upright stress

NATURAL PARTNERS

• This font shares many of the qualities of the sans serif font **Bell Centennial**. For a complete contrast, try **Centennial**.

FONT FEATURES

● The 'S' has a completely different angle of stress to all other characters

● The tail of the 'Q' is longer within the counter than it is outside

Deep Capitals

ABCDEF
GHIJKL
MNOPQR
STUVWX
YZ

DEEP CAPITALS

a b c d e f
g h i j k l
m n o p q r
s t u v w x
y z

DRAW YOUR OWN

TOPIARY

Vanessa Hamilton is obviously good in the garden as well as the home (see Knit, page 36). This jolly collection of leafy characters could double up as clouds too, so you're covered for the air display as well as the local flower show. Character angles can be adjusted for different character pairings.

ANATOMY OF THE FONT

Surprisingly legible despite the large amount of decorative detailing, Topiary is a proportional display font with obvious applications (see above) and a great sense of fun. Try very close character spacing to form a kind of typographic hedge.

KEY FONT DETAILS

• The angled stress is completely random and fully adjustable for all glyphs
• Stem widths are consistent from glyph to glyph despite random shaping

NATURAL PARTNERS

• The letterforms of this illustrated font are in fact surprisingly consistent geometrically – the 'O' for example is circular. The obvious partner here is Futura as it shares very similar consistent qualities.

FONT FEATURES

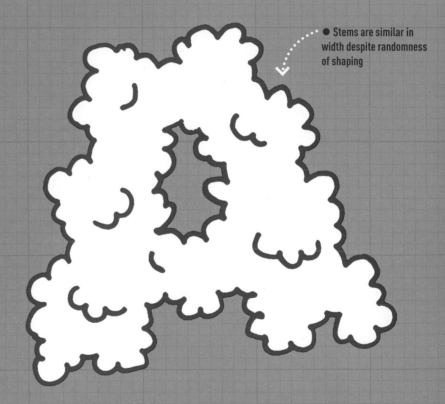

● Stems are similar in width despite randomness of shaping

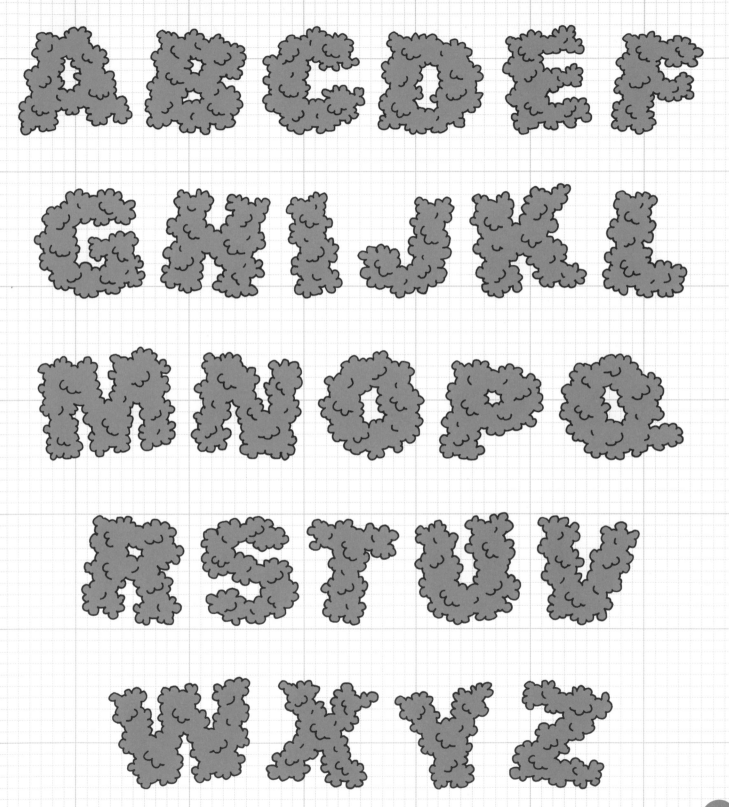

DRAW YOUR OWN

FILLED PATTERN

This distinctly retro font by an emerging young designer is based on the once maligned, but newly cool, Cooper Black typeface. Born from a love of excessive scribbling, the pattern has a kind of 1970s pop magazine meets the Grateful Dead look. Younger readers can resort to Google if that means nothing to them.

ANATOMY OF THE FONT

The use of Cooper Black as the main outline for this kitsch-pop font is spot on as the chunky serifs and voluptuous curves are made to accommodate the patterns and added decoration. Cooper Black was actually designed in the 1920s, but curiously looks very 1970s in style.

KEY FONT DETAILS

• Decorative embellishments vary between characters, with some carrying only patterned fill within the main outline

NATURAL PARTNERS

• To keep the fun retro theme going, you could try pairing with **Souvenir**, another font that's regained a degree of popularity in recent years. Alternatively, take a look at the expanded weights of **Folio**.

FONT FEATURES

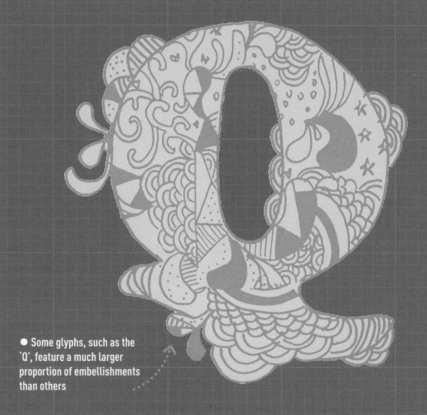

● Some glyphs, such as the 'Q', feature a much larger proportion of embellishments than others

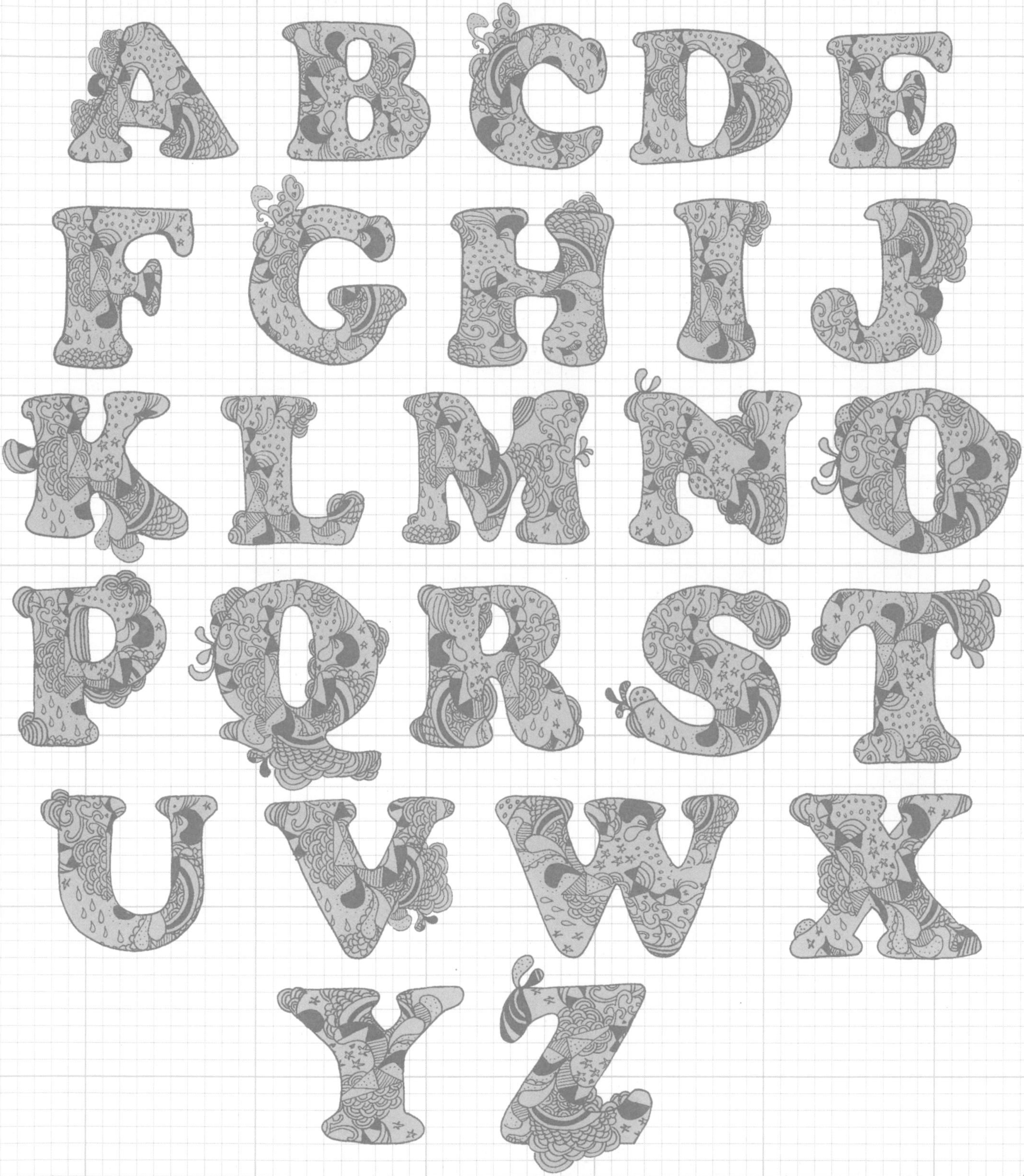
ABCDE
FGHIJ
KLMNO
PQRST
UVWX
YZ

FILLED PATTERN

Inspired by other retro bands? Create your own unique filled pattern.

DRAW YOUR OWN

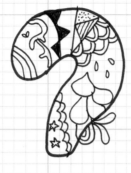

PATTERN FRONT

The aura emanating from the characters of this typeface were inspired by the pattern that this illustrator doodles when she's speaking to someone on the phone. The tightly-packed circles suggest movement and could work well if animated. Great for injecting some fun into the everyday.

ANATOMY OF THE FONT

The relatively standard letterforms that make up this typeface are not overpowered by the patterning. When creating patterned typefaces, it's advisable to start with a boldly structured character set which can carry the level of decorative additions.

KEY FONT DETAILS

• The patterning dictates the need for very loose character spacing
• The counters are clear as the pattern follows the edges

NATURAL PARTNERS

• Because the pattern detail extends outside the main letterform, a delicate slab serif such as **Officina Serif** will work alongside this decorative font. Pair it with **Officina Sans** for an all-round fit.

FONT FEATURES

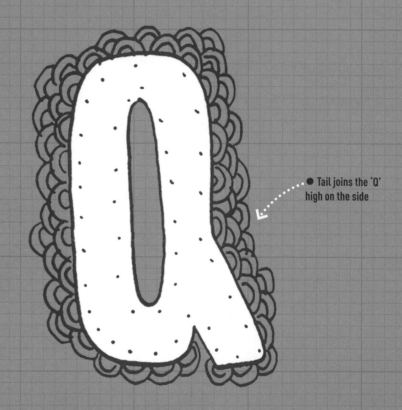

● Tail joins the 'Q' high on the side

PATTERN FRONT

A B C D E F
G H I J K L
M N O P Q R
S T U V W
X Y Z

abcdefghij
klmnopqrs
tuvwxyz
ôüßÉãñ
?!$€€%@.,

DRAW YOUR OWN

TIME 74

Handwriting is, of course, a great source of inspiration for hand-drawn fonts. Time 74 is styled after designer Lee Suttey's signature, which features a double crossed 'T'. Adding detail to the ascenders and descenders solved the problem of what to do with characters that have no cross strokes.

ANATOMY OF THE FONT

Sometimes less is most definitely more when it comes to creating successful hand lettering, and Time 74 is a prime example of this. The simple addition of a series of double strokes transforms the relatively basic letterforms into something much more unusual.

KEY FONT DETAILS

• The capital 'A' has no horizontal stroke
• Selected lower case characters echo the form of their upper case equivalent

NATURAL PARTNERS

• This rather elegant font deserves to be paired with a no-nonsense sans serif that won't jar, so try News Gothic. A quietly sophisticated font such as Caecilia, with its subtle detailing, will also work.

FONT FEATURES

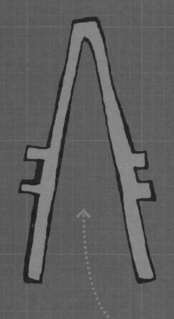

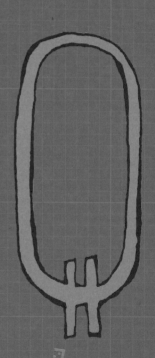

● The 'A' lacks a crossbar

● The tail of the 'Q' is formed from the decorative double stroke of the other glyphs

ABCDEFGHIJ
KLMNOPQRS
TUVWXYZ
ÑÜBÉĂÔÏÇ
1234567890

ABCDEFGHIJK
Lmnopqrst
uvwxyz?¿!¡
(ñÑÜÜßÉĚŁÔïïiÇ)
@$≠%£‚‚‚‚‚==
=

DRAW YOUR OWN

SPAGHETTI JUNCTION

This aptly named font by Michelle Tilly is arguably the most complex in the book to draw, but it's easier than it appears due to its free-form nature. Imagine each character looking different every time you slap a handful of pasta onto the counter-top. Start from a corner and work into the curves for the best results.

ANATOMY OF THE FONT

This is arguably the ultimate typeface for people who love to doodle, and essentially each character can be subtly changed every time you draw it. The key for drawing this kind of free-form lettering is to work to a consistent chosen outline, preferably a bold display font.

KEY FONT DETAILS

- Where to start – every character contains some unique features, variants of stroke width and level of detail
- Some characters (such as 'R' and 'S') join when paired, but can also function as standalone glyphs if required

NATURAL PARTNERS

- This is a category-defying font, but it's built around a strong basic geometry, so why not pair it with **Futura**?

FONT FEATURES

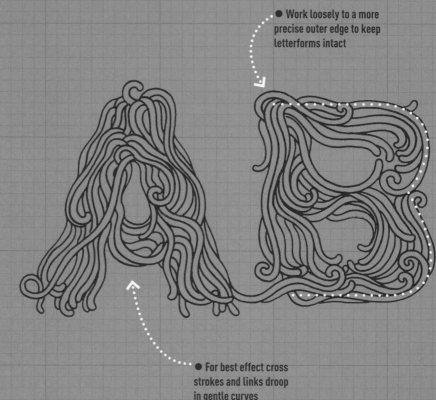

● Work loosely to a more precise outer edge to keep letterforms intact

● For best effect cross strokes and links droop in gentle curves

ABCDEFG
HIJKLMN
OPQRST
UVWXY
YZ

SPAGHETTI JUNCTION

Mealtimes will never be the same again ...

DRAW YOUR OWN

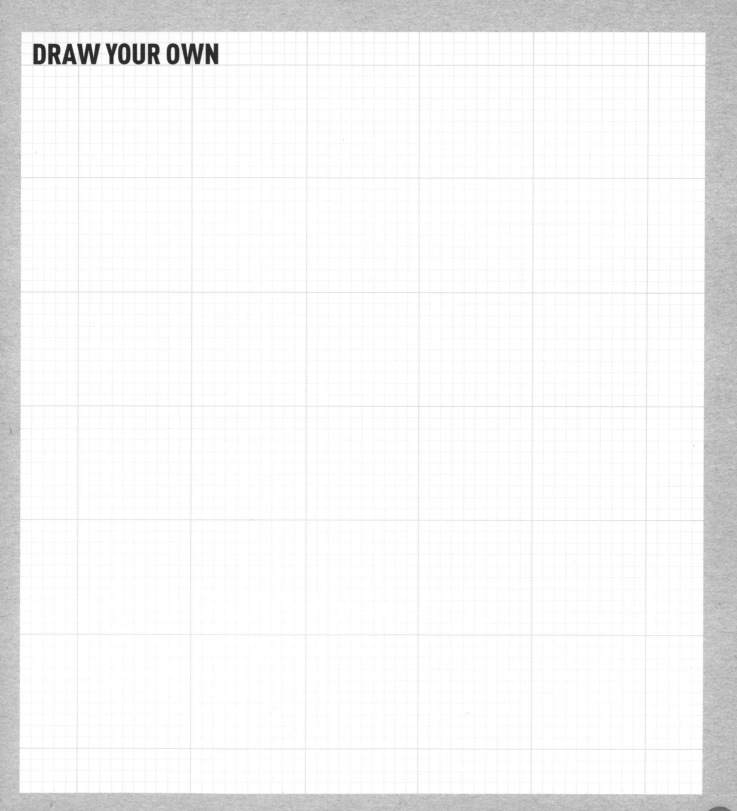

SLOWWORM

Have you ever read 'How to Eat Fried Worms' by Thomas Rockwell? As a child (and presumably still now) Tonwen Jones held a great fondness for the book, which provided the inspiration for this font. For variety, try switching the position of the heads and tails to create alternative characters.

ANATOMY OF THE FONT

This font appears at first glance to be very loosely drawn, but in fact there's more structure to the characters than meets the eye. A great fun font for children, readability is very important for developing minds and Slowworm's clear letterforms are highly legible. An easy font to get you started.

KEY FONT DETAILS

• Characters formed from a single 'worm' break without forming closed counters
• The capital 'P' contains a sharp corner whilst other characters are more rounded

NATURAL PARTNERS

• The rounded stroke endings of Slowworm provide us with a clue to a good typographic partner. For headings try **Bryant** or perhaps **Cholla Sans** for running text.

FONT FEATURES

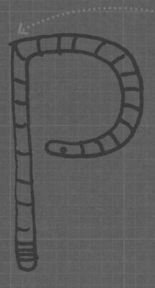

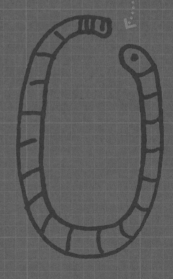

● The 'P' features an angled corner while other glyphs are more rounded

● Several glyphs feature open bowls or counters

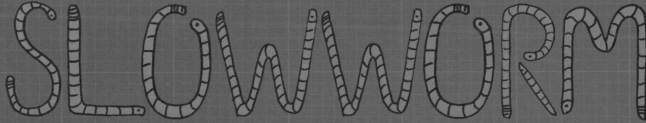

ABCDEF
GHIJKL
MNOPQR
STUVW
XYZ

DRAW YOUR OWN

BULK

During a holiday in Sydney, Australia, Wayne Blades was browsing in furniture store Orson & Blake when he sketched a chair and table that reminded him of three-dimensional letterforms. The plan was to take a course and make the expensive furniture himself one day – maybe this font will kick-start that ambition?

ANATOMY OF THE FONT

The characters of this font are cut from virtual blocks using 90° angles throughout, so no curved surfaces feature in any of the glyphs. The challenge this presents in terms of differentiating between similar characters such as the 'U' and 'V' is addressed through the application of varying stroke widths.

KEY FONT DETAILS

• The 'A' is completely solid between its apex and horizontal stroke

• Certain characters, such as the 'D' and 'E', lack vertical strokes

NATURAL PARTNERS

• As this font is so solid and imposing, a serif with a classic feel will pair well. For running text try Bembo, or Mrs Eaves which has an unusually short x-height.

FONT FEATURES

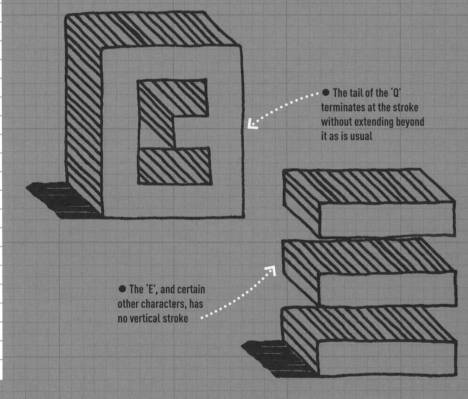

● The tail of the 'Q' terminates at the stroke without extending beyond it as is usual

● The 'E', and certain other characters, has no vertical stroke

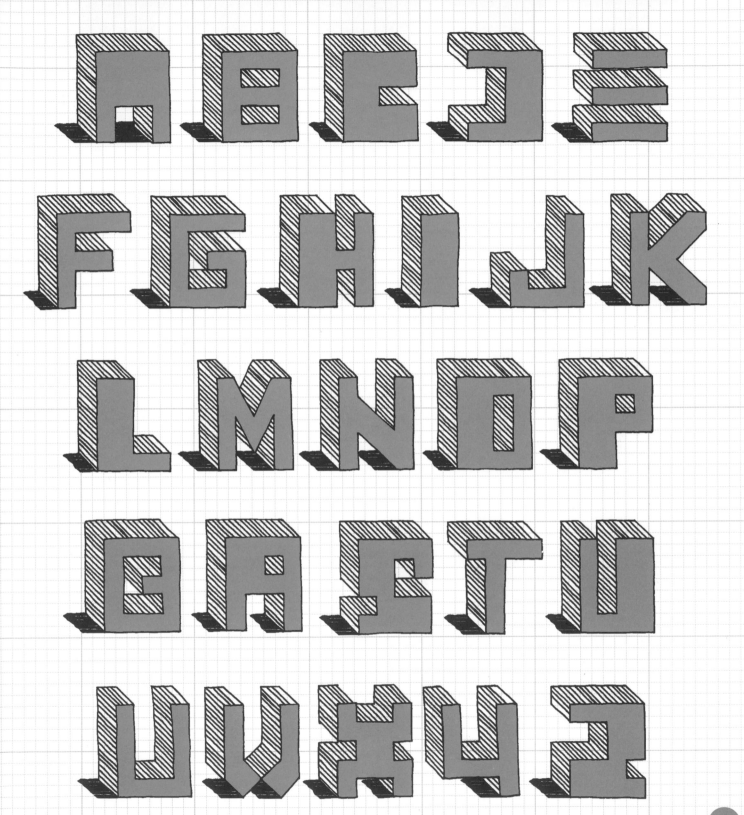

BULK

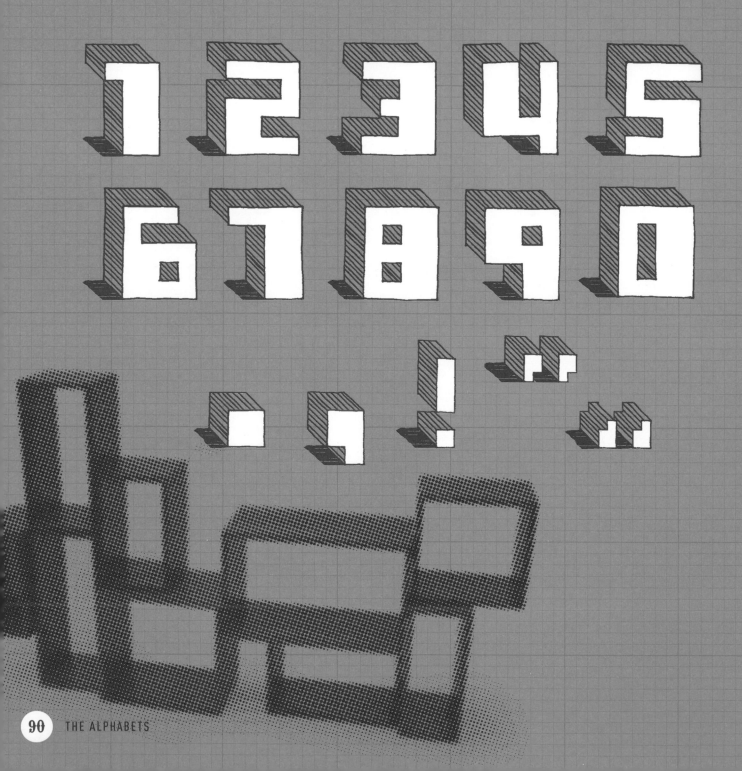

DRAW YOUR OWN

HAIRY BEAST

If there were ever a typeface that would look great in an illustrated children's book about, well, hairy things, then this is it. The inspiration actually came from the illustrator's flatmate, who had particularly hairy toes. Yuck! Too much information, I think, but the font is very cute.

FONT FEATURES

ANATOMY OF THE FONT

The character of this humorous font lies mainly in the hairy decoration and the addition of toes at the terminals, but the irregular qualities of the strokes also add a sense of warmth and friendliness to the styling.

KEY FONT DETAILS

• The tail of the capital 'Q' crosses into the counter
• The instroke of the capital 'G' noticeably overhangs the stem

NATURAL PARTNERS

• Given that this is such an obvious candidate for use with material for children, partner fonts should exhibit a high level of readability. A simple font such as VAG Rounded will work, as will the extremely versatile Frutiger.

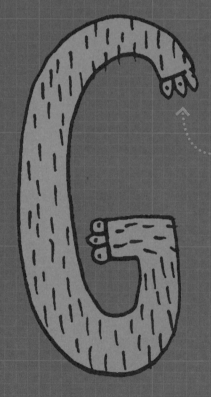

● There is a significant overhang on the instroke of the 'G'

A B C D E F

G H I J K L

M N O P Q R

S T U V W

X Y Z

Replace those toes with teeth for a scarier-looking beast...

DRAW YOUR OWN

SPOTTY FAIRGROUND

Vintage signage on a local pier provided the starting point for Michelle Tilly's fairground-influenced font. The added dots are designed to resemble the lights found on old fairground rides, but they also make the characters look like the escutcheon plates on an old lock, or even the detail on a suit of armour.

ANATOMY OF THE FONT

The characters of this vintage font appear to be cut from sheet metal or perhaps plywood, which is likely to be true of the original typeface that influenced the design. Try adding some alternative colours to the dots for extra zing.

KEY FONT DETAILS

- The vertices at the base of the capital 'W' are outfacing
- Horizontal strokes on the 'E', 'F' and 'L' are slightly curved

NATURAL PARTNERS

- Don't be tempted to pair this font with any of the gimmicky vintage fonts that crop up on free font websites. Use a vintage font with a genuine pedigree, such as **Clarendon** or the original Baskerville.

FONT FEATURES

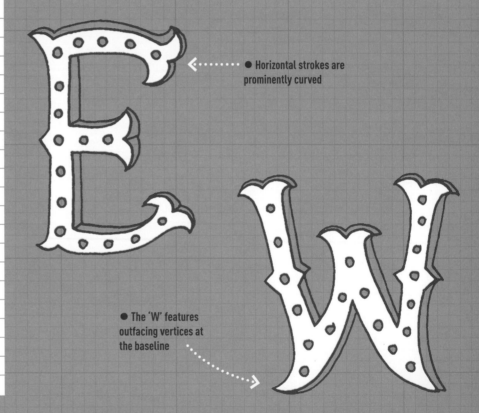

● Horizontal strokes are prominently curved

● The 'W' features outfacing vertices at the baseline

SPOTTY FAIRGROUND

ABCDEF
GHIJKL
MNOPQR
STUVWX
YZ

SPOTTY FAIRGROUND

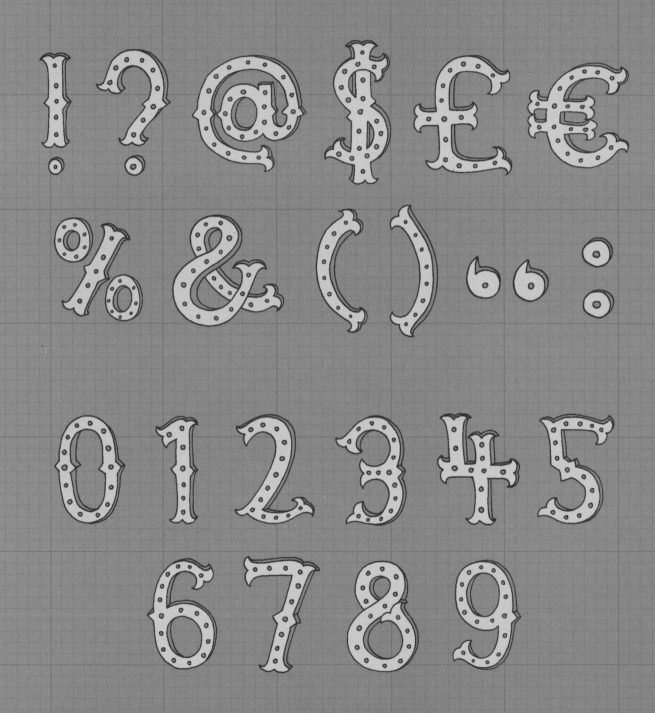

DRAW YOUR OWN

CARNIVAL FREEHAND

Based on the well-known font Rosewood, this hand-drawn version is at a glance quite similar to the original, but take a closer look and you'll realize that the loose qualities of the redraw have injected a different feel to the characters. The irregular line quality is much more 'seedy carnival' than 'shiny showman'.

ANATOMY OF THE FONT

The classic fairground font is revisited here as a rougher carnival sideshow with its looser hand-drawn styling. The patterning on the strokes could be recoloured with bright primaries for the traditional look, or with even brighter neon colours to evoke a more contemporary feel.

KEY FONT DETAILS

• The 'G' has a fully closed aperture, reflecting the influence of **ROSEWOOD** on the design

• The cap 'R' has a prominent upturned tail

NATURAL PARTNERS

• Like the previous font, Spotty Fairground, Carnival Freehand should be paired with another face that's the genuine article. Take a look at Caslon or Granjon, the latter being a later revival of Garamond.

FONT FEATURES

● The 'G' has a fully closed aperture instead of the usual gap

● Looser linework changes the character of the original typeface

CARNIVAL FREEHAND

A B C D E F
G H I J K L
M N O P Q R
S T U V W X
Y Z

CARNIVAL FREEHAND

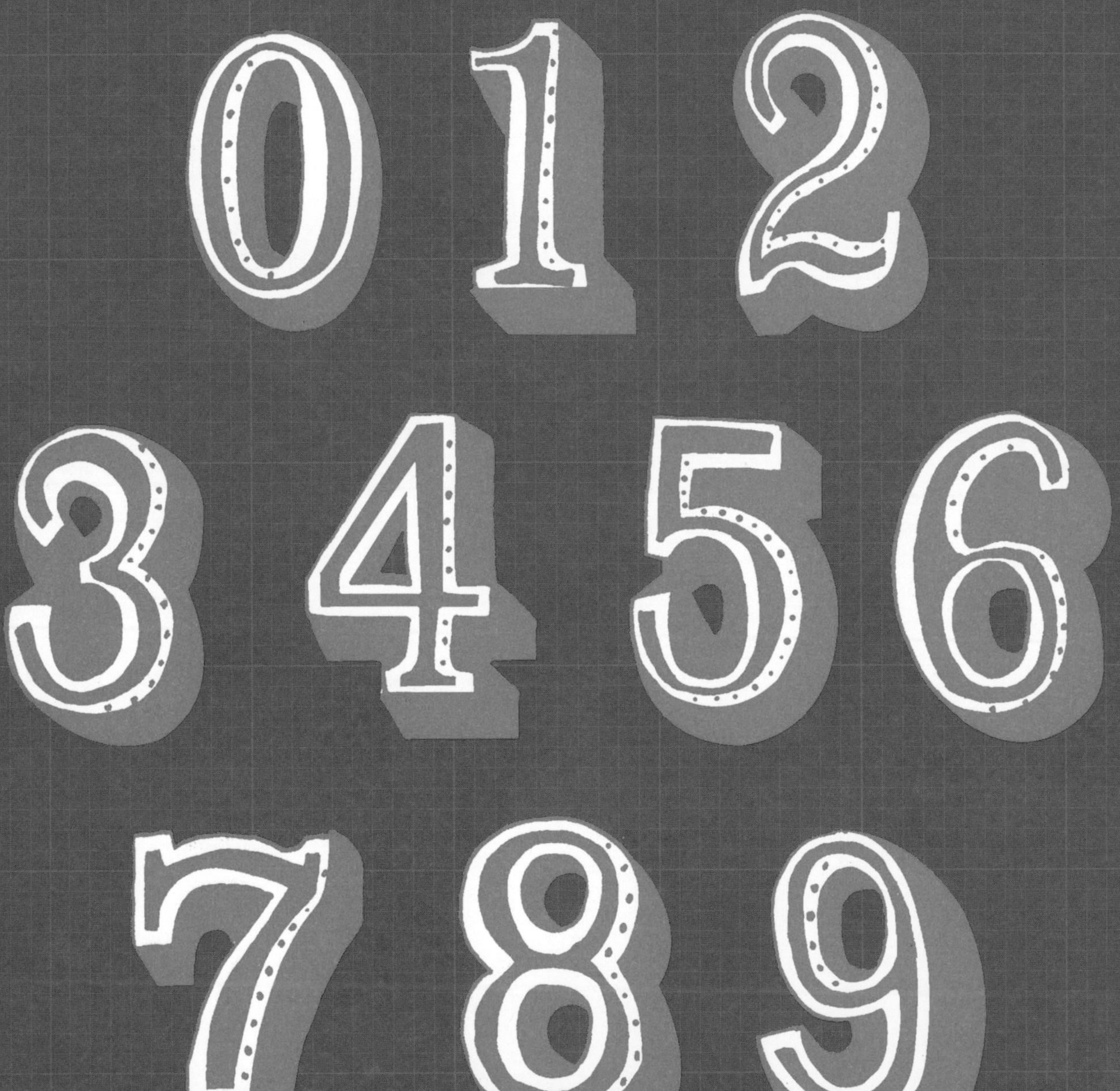

DRAW YOUR OWN

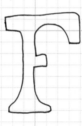

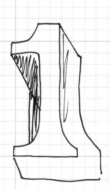

SEVEN O'CLOCK SHADOW

Dave Pentland is fortunate to work in a sea-front studio in Brighton, UK, and early one evening he noticed shadows creeping up the walls of some nearby Victorian buildings as the sun set. A simple script font that he was working on at the time immediately morphed into Seven O'Clock Shadow.

ANATOMY OF THE FONT

The forward-angled stress of this casually amorphous font gives away its origins as a more formal script face. The caps show a weight bias to the left, whilst the lower case letters tend towards being slightly bottom heavy, anchoring the characters solidly to the baseline.

KEY FONT DETAILS

• The cap 'W' features a very low central apex that almost merges with the outer stems

• The stems to the left of each character are much thicker than those on the right

NATURAL PARTNERS

• This is a font with a lot of visual presence, so complementary fonts need to exhibit a distinct contrast. You can use the weight of a font like **Unit Black** or Unit Light to achieve this contrast.

FONT FEATURES

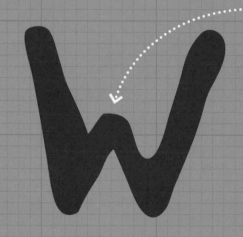

• The middle apex of the 'W' is very short compared with the cap height

• Lower case characters exhibit a distinct increase in stem weight nearer the baseline

SEVEN O'CLOCK SHADOW

ABCDEFG
HIJKLMN
OPQRST
UVWXYZ
.?!@£":$()

abcdefg
hijklmn
opqrstu
vwxyz

àéôïñüçß

DRAW YOUR OWN

ABRUPTURE

Scott Suttey was attempting to conjure a rough but traditionally structured font when he created Abrupture. He drew a standardized set of character segments, then scanned them and pieced each character together using Adobe Illustrator. Cap heights vary but the baseline is a constant.

ANATOMY OF THE FONT

This well proportioned and carefully constructed font gives the impression of being taller than it actually is. The raised cross strokes and coordinating small counters draw the eye towards the upper portions of the characters, conveying an elegance around the face.

KEY FONT DETAILS

• The 'V' features an upright stem rather than the more usual pair of diagonal strokes
• The leg of the 'K' begins as a horizontal cross stroke

NATURAL PARTNERS

• Because this font appears so tall, it's a neat typographic trick to use a partner font with a low x-height as a contrast. Try Eureka Sans or Kievit.

FONT FEATURES

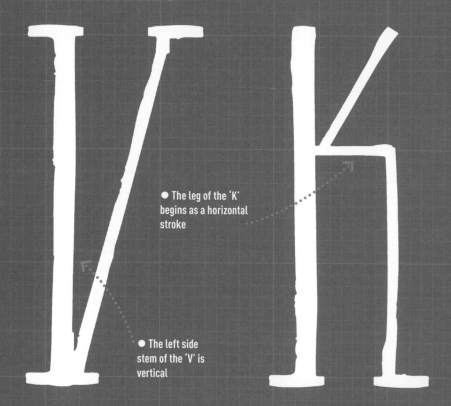

● The leg of the 'K' begins as a horizontal stroke

● The left side stem of the 'V' is vertical

ABRUPTURE

ABCDEFGHIJK
LMNOPQRST
UVWXYZ
ÀÇÉÏÑÔÜß
1234567890

ABRUPTURE

abcdefghijk
lmnopqrst
uvwxyz
àçëïñôüß ﬀ ﬄ ﬃ
!?@$&%£;"":.()

DRAW YOUR OWN

hello

LEPIDOPTERA

There's something distinctly insect-like about this font's qualities, explained by the fact that Tonwen Jones took inspiration from the antennae of butterflies when creating the scrolls that adjoin the spines and stems. The added patterning on the stems enhances the elegance of this attractive font.

ANATOMY OF THE FONT

Lepidoptera is one of the more calligraphic fonts featured in this book. The flowing curls, designed to look like insect antennae, give this face a distinctly ornate feel.

KEY FONT DETAILS

• The 'G' doesn't feature a cross stroke
• Selected characters such as the 'U' and 'V' only feature one stem

NATURAL PARTNERS

• Although instinct dictates that a contrasting sans serif would work as a partner for this delicate font, try working with a light serif when using Lepidoptera with running text. Look specifically at **Bodoni** or Didot which have very fine serifs.

FONT FEATURES

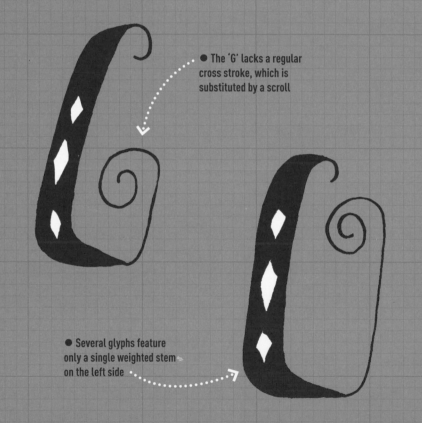

• The 'G' lacks a regular cross stroke, which is substituted by a scroll

• Several glyphs feature only a single weighted stem on the left side

A B C D E F
G H I J K L
M N O P Q R
S T U V W
X Y Z

LEPIDOPTERA

DRAW YOUR OWN

CRESCENT

A case of illustrator's block was holding up the creative process for Holly Sellors until she caught a glimpse of the dark yellow crescent moon through the window. The relatively fine curves and crescent shapes that make up the characters of this font are a reflection of that inspiring view.

ANATOMY OF THE FONT

The irregular character shapes of this font are formed largely from overlaid crescents with one flat side. This creates the interesting juxtaposition of very rounded outer letterforms with the angular squared counters. Lower case characters link in a similar way to a more traditional script face.

KEY FONT DETAILS

• Every stem and stroke is slightly different in either weight or form

• Counters are squared within rounded forms

NATURAL PARTNERS

• You'll need to select a partner with a lot of presence to measure up to this very bold font. Try the well-known **Gill Sans**, or perhaps the very flexible **Interstate**.

FONT FEATURES

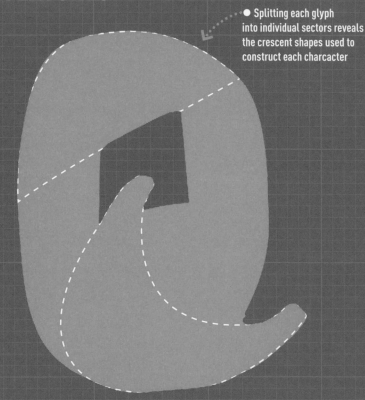

● Splitting each glyph into individual sectors reveals the crescent shapes used to construct each charcacter

CRESCENT

ABCDEF
GHIJKL
MNOPQR
STUVW
XYZ

CRESCENT

abcdefghij

klmnopqr

stuvwxyz

1234567890

(!?@&$£%;:)

DRAW YOUR OWN

SCRIPT TWO

The very idea of a script font conjures up visions of dip pens and ink wells, and those very items provided the inspiration for this elegantly flowing alphabet. As with much of Tonwen Jones' work, the shaping of the letterforms are also linked closely to her illustration style.

ANATOMY OF THE FONT

This calligraphic font with a light touch is a good example of how a hand-drawn font can act as a representation of the designer's style of handwriting. Characters are elegantly calligraphic, with plenty of contrast between the thick and thin strokes.

KEY FONT DETAILS

• Stems are never vertical or straight, and in the case of the 'E' the stem is missing altogether
• Loops are used at junctions where a thin stroke and a thick stroke meet

NATURAL PARTNERS

• Script Two would benefit from a pairing with a contrasting sans serif. Take a look at either Benton Sans or Dax.

FONT FEATURES

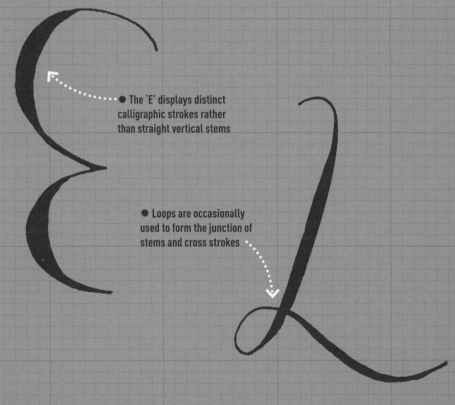

• The 'E' displays distinct calligraphic strokes rather than straight vertical stems

• Loops are occasionally used to form the junction of stems and cross strokes

A B C D E F

G H I J K L

M N O P Q R

S T U U W

X Y Z & $ £ @ ?

ab cd ef gh ij

kl mn op qr st

u v w x y z

1 2 3 4 5

6 7 8 9

DRAW YOUR OWN

BLACKOUT

Creating a script font with a twist isn't the easiest task one could set oneself, as it's generally accepted that a script should be derived from either an historical or modern handwriting style. However, combining a traditional script letterform with a significant 'extra' feature such as filling counters can work.

ANATOMY OF THE FONT

The filled areas of this fun font tend to jump out at you before the shape of the whole character: the main strokes are fairly light, so only selected areas are solid. This helps to make each glyph distinct and aids readability.

KEY FONT DETAILS

• The 'M' lacks scrolls (unlike the 'A' or 'N') at the foot of each stem
• The majority of characters are formed from one unbroken stroke – exceptions being the 'D', 'Q' and 'T'

NATURAL PARTNERS

• A sans serif with the kind of flowing characteristics demonstrated by Blackout will work well here. **TheSans** does just this, and has a very large range of weights to choose from too.

FONT FEATURES

● Areas are filled selectively in order to aid character recognition

● Certain characters with fewer opportunities for detailing are filled entirely

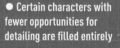

A B C D E F

G H I J K L

M N O P Q R

S T U V W X

Y Z £ $ £ @ ?

BLACKOUT

a b cd ef g hij kl
mn op qr st u
vw x y z
1 2 3 4 5
6 7 8 9

DRAW YOUR OWN

OCTOBET

A recent illustration graduate from the University of Brighton, Alex Wells took her inspiration for this slightly sinister and highly detailed font from an ancient Norse legend. The Kraken was supposedly an enormous octopus-like creature that once lived off the coasts of Norway and Greenland.

ANATOMY OF THE FONT

The Victorians loved to create illustrative fonts using organic forms, and Octobet wouldn't look out of place in a book of late 19th-century ephemera. However, the intricate surface detailing makes this font feel much more contemporary than the woodcuts of old.

KEY FONT DETAILS

• The circular (or near circular) characters 'D', 'O' and 'Q' are visually quite similar
• Surface detail varies considerably between each separate glyph

NATURAL PARTNERS

• A classically proportioned serif face is an ideal partner for a font of this kind. Perpetua is based on a clean, engraved lettering style and won't fight against the high level of detail in Octobet.

FONT FEATURES

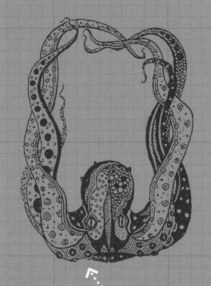

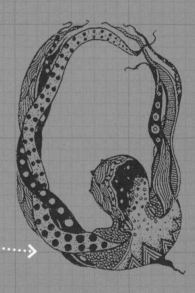

● The 'O' and 'Q' are very similar – the 'Q' being slightly rotated to indicate a cross stroke

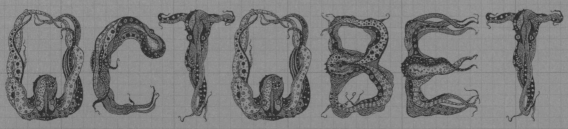

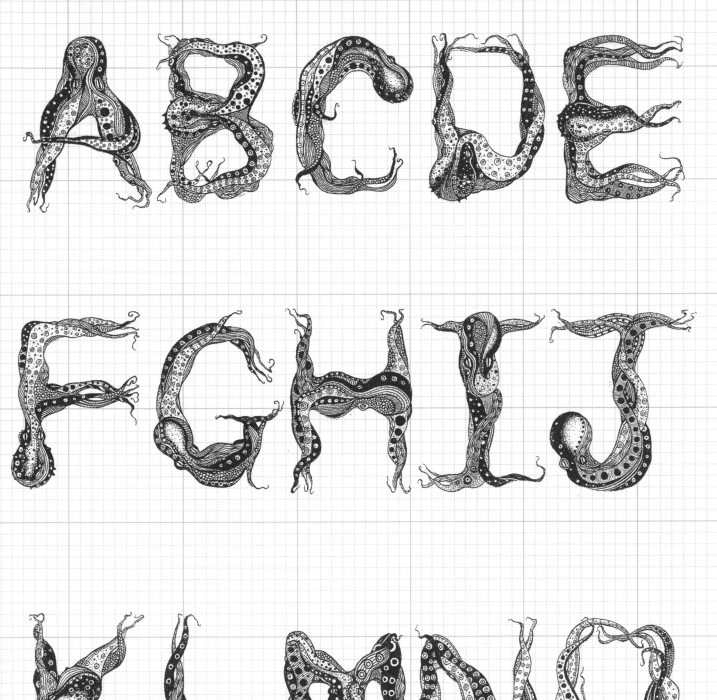

DRAW YOUR OWN

KATIE'S HAND

Aside from her first love, photography and image-making, Katie Greenwood also holds a passion for design and typography and came up with this handwriting font whilst brainstorming a design for a relaxed cursive script. It closely echoes Katie's handwriting, hence the name, but is apparently somewhat neater!

ANATOMY OF THE FONT

Like Script Two (see page 120), Katie's Hand emulates the designer's handwriting, but in this case the result is closer to a more 'every day' writing style as there is little contrast in stroke widths. Think of this more as a handwriting font written with a standard marker rather than a calligraphic pen.

KEY FONT DETAILS

• The forward-leaning stress of the characters imply that the designer is right-handed

• Characters with a single stem (with the exception of the 'P') do not have outward-facing feet

NATURAL PARTNERS

• As a more straightforward handwriting font, Katie's Hand can be paired successfully with a broader range of fonts. Try a sans serif such as Avenir or a serif such as Garamond.

FONT FEATURES

M

● The lower apex of the 'M' doesn't reach the baseline

A

● Feet turn outwards on several characters with vertical or diagonal stems

KATIE'S HAND

ABCDEFG
HIJKLMN
OPQRSTU
VWXYZ
!@£$%.^*().,

abcdef
ghijklm
nopqrs
tuvwxyz
1234567890

DRAW YOUR OWN

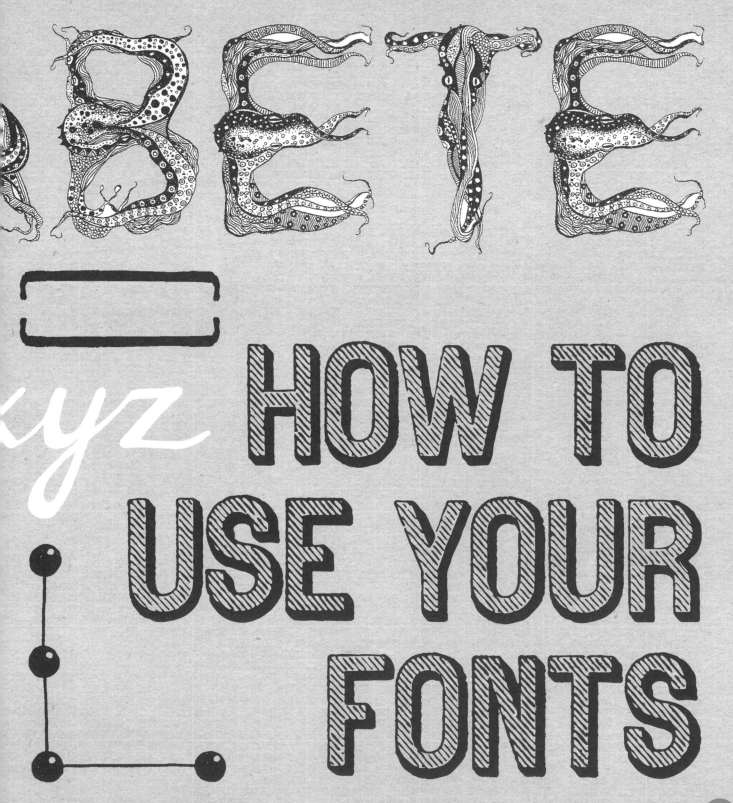

HOW TO USE YOUR FONTS

HOW COMPUTERS HANDLE FONTS

First of all, let's clarify the difference between a font and a typeface, as it's a common misconception that they're the same thing. A font is all the characters, or more precisely glyphs, of a typeface, including the numerals, punctuation, and various other symbols, at a specific point size and weight. A typeface is the collection of all of the point sizes and all of the weights from a font family.

For example, **Rockwell** (see page 16) is a *typeface*, but **11 point Rockwell Bold** (fonts are measured in points) is a *font*. Put another way, the typeface is the overall design, whereas the font is the electronic code that gets installed on your Mac or PC in order to allow type to render on the screen and print through your inkjet.

OK, that's all very well, but how do the fonts actually work?

In the early days of computing fonts were bitmapped, meaning that a separate little image of each character or glyph had to be created for each point size. If you wanted to display a font at a size which didn't correspond to the bitmaps included with the font, the characters would be jagged at the edges, and printed text usually looked ugly.

Around the middle of the 1980s, Adobe introduced PostScript Type 1 fonts. These changed everything, as PostScript fonts were based on scalable vectors instead of bitmaps; in other words, PostScript didn't have to rely on little images for each character anymore. *We talk about vectors in more detail on the next spread, by the way.* This meant that a single, vector-based image of each character could generate accurately rendered type at any point size. Around the same time, Adobe also adapted PostScript so it could be used as the language utilized by computers to transmit pages to a laser printer, all of which helped make the desktop publishing revolution possible. Huzzah! PostScript Type 1 fonts came in two parts, a screen font and a printer font and both have to be installed on your system if the font is to work properly. They are still very much in use today but are essentially old technology or 'legacy software'.

Apple liked what was going on with this technology but didn't want to share with Adobe so they got together with Microsoft to develop their own vector font and printing technology. Apple came up with TrueType whilst Microsoft worked on a print engine they called Trueimage, which never

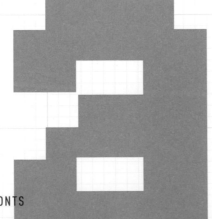

65,536

You probably won't need to use every one of the 65,536 glyph options available through OpenType for your own hand-drawn font projects! The font shown is Abrupture by Scott Suttey (see page 108).

took off and was subsequently dropped. TrueType fonts were, and to a large extent still are, very successful and once again thousands of them are still around and in common use. A TrueType font consists of a single data file per weight, whilst Mac and Windows operating systems include the software needed to render the font.

The defacto technology for scalable fonts now is OpenType, which owes a lot to TrueType in terms of basic functionality. This time it was Microsoft

and Adobe that got together, and the platform sports numerous advantages over previous font technologies. The stand-out advantage is that a single OpenType font can contain 65,536 glyphs in its single data file instead of the meagre 256 glyphs that the old Type 1 fonts could manage – great news for the Chinese!

BITMAP VERSUS VECTOR

When it comes to scalable fonts, vectors are the runaway winner because of that word 'scalable'. 'You can scale bitmaps', I hear you say, and you'd be right, but with fonts it's all about quality, and vectors have the ability to provide the highest quality for type scaled up theoretically to infinite sizes.

A bitmap is made from pixels. Bitmaps handle tonal gradations and colour blends very well so are great for photorealistic images, but are resolution-dependent. Images appearing in print must be around 300ppi (which means a resolution of 300 pixels per inch) to be of sufficient quality. Screen images for websites can be a lot lower, at around 72ppi. Because they're resolution-dependent, they're not infinitely scalable as any enlargement produces a corresponding loss in quality.

Vectors, on the other hand, are not at all resolution-dependent as they use geometrical primitives *(which are pretty much what the word implies – basic geometric objects)* such as points, lines, curves

A vector outline of the 'Q' from the font Adobe Caslon, showing active adjustment points and handles.

Aa Aa Ta Ta

36 point   236 point   536 point

and polygons. A vector is made from lines rather than pixels, and a mathematical equation calculates all the points of intersection and the shapes between those points. This means that when you resize a vector, the exact shape is simply recalculated and redrawn at the size you wish to use it. Vectors aren't the best choice of format when creating photorealistic images as the line-based construction doesn't lend itself well to subtle shifts in colour, although surprisingly good results can be achieved all the same, depending on the content of the image. However, they're perfect for things like logotypes and technical illustrations, and of course for fonts. The scalable properties of a vector means the same font can be set at 6 point, 60 point or 600 point with no loss in quality whatsoever.

There's another big advantage provided by vectors – file size. Think about a line drawn as a bitmap and you have a series of aligned pixels with each pixel taking up a small amount of data. The longer the line gets, the more pixels you need to add, and the more data you need in order to draw the line. Now think about a line drawn as a vector. It's never going to be more than two points

no matter how long the line gets, so in this respect vector files are a great deal smaller than bitmap files. This is why type designers are able to keep the file sizes of their fonts relatively small.

Do remember that ultimately computers and printers have to convert everything into a bitmap because they're digital so everything is made up of pixels, and what you see on screen or on paper is never truly a vector. What you see is a 'rasterized' version of the vector, which you can think of as a very accurate preview. The vector is converted to pixels, with the resolution of that conversion limited to the maximum resolution of your computer screen or printer. The point is, it's converted at actual size every time so the quality of the output is never compromised.

DRAWING & SCANNING FONTS

The first thing to say about drawing a font is that there's no one prescribed method, but there are a couple of things you can do to help ensure impressive results. First of all, use good quality paper with a smooth surface that won't snag your pen as you draw. Also, try to use paper that has a low absorption level so it doesn't ruck up and distort the letterforms when you use pen and ink.

Personally, I find the quality of paper in higher-end layout pads good for drawing, but it's worth experimenting with a few different types of stock to find the one that suits you best. Secondly, use the right drawing tool for the style of lettering you want to create. Sketching letterforms with a pencil before working over the top with a pen or marker is a good way to start, but if you want something calligraphic try using a calligraphy pen straight away. Fine-liners are great for inking over pencil and flow nicely over the paper surface for smooth curves and lines; and if you want a marker pen for heavier line work, look no further than a good old Sharpie – they're the best.

I mentioned at the beginning of the book that if you want to create a full set of characters for further use rather than a one-off piece, do your best to maintain the same scale when you're drawing your original characters prior to scanning. It's not that easy to pull everything together at the same size if you don't do this, and line weights will vary if you have to scale individual characters up or down.

OK, so let's assume you've got a bunch of hand-drawn characters ready for scanning. The best bit of advice I can give you here is to work as cleanly as possible. If you haven't used your scanner for a while, give the glass a good polish before you start, and use an eraser to remove any unwanted sketch lines from the original. Remember I mentioned blue pencils back on page 8? If you use a blue pencil to create your sketch lines, the scanner won't pick them up (unless they're overly heavy), so consider this as an option.

You can scan originals as a black-and-white bitmap immediately, given that ultimately your characters have to consist only of solid areas. You don't want any shades of grey in there as we're going to turn these characters into vectors next. However, I would recommend scanning as a greyscale first in order to collect as much detail as possible, followed by a clean-up prior to the vector drawing stage. Go for a high-resolution setting on your scanner, certainly no lower than 300dpi. I normally scan line work at 600dpi to ensure I pick up every detail.

Once you've completed scanning, open up the images in image-editing software such as Photoshop Elements to check for unwanted detail. The easiest way to remove stray specs and lines is to use the Levels Adjustment (Enhance > Adjust Lighting > Levels) to adjust the contrast, making

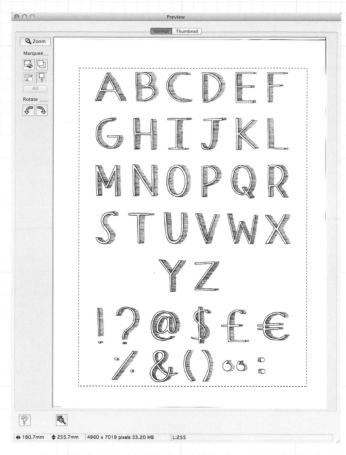

Check that you're scanning in Grayscale (8-bit is fine for this purpose), and make sure the resolution is set to at least 300 dpi. The font shown here is Skinny Fringe by Michelle Tilly (see page 44).

the whites whiter and the blacks blacker. You can't adjust the contrast of a bitmap, hence my advice to start with a greyscale scan. Once you're happy with the scan, you're ready to start drawing your character.

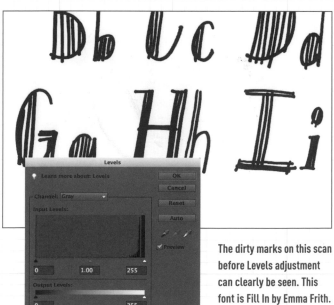

The dirty marks on this scan before Levels adjustment can clearly be seen. This font is Fill In by Emma Frith. (see page 40).

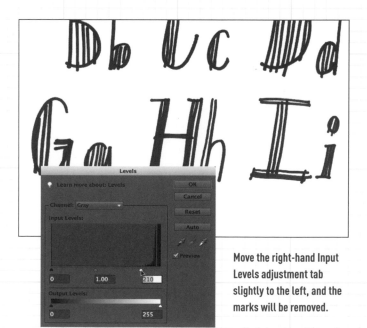

Move the right-hand Input Levels adjustment tab slightly to the left, and the marks will be removed.

DRAWING WITH VECTORS

In the context of this book, we're faced with two options for digitizing our new hand-drawn characters. We can take our scan and do a straight auto-trace, which is quick and easy and perfectly acceptable for this kind of work. Alternatively, we can use the scan as a guide and redraw our characters manually using the tools available to us in our chosen software package.

I'll be using Adobe Illustrator CS6 but the methods described here can be followed with any of the popular vector-capable applications currently available, and they're much easier than you might think at first.

Auto-tracing with Adobe Illustrator

Let's kick off by talking about auto-trace. Adobe Illustrator is capable of tracing a scanned image with a very high degree of accuracy and comes with a useful collection of presets so you don't even have to puzzle over the various settings. Open your scan directly within Illustrator and click on the small arrow to the right of the Image Trace button in the Toolbar at the top of the screen. If you're working with a version of Illustrator earlier than CS6, this button is labelled Live Trace. You'll see a variety of presets listed here, so experiment by clicking on each one in turn to see what you get, using the undo command where necessary. In CS6

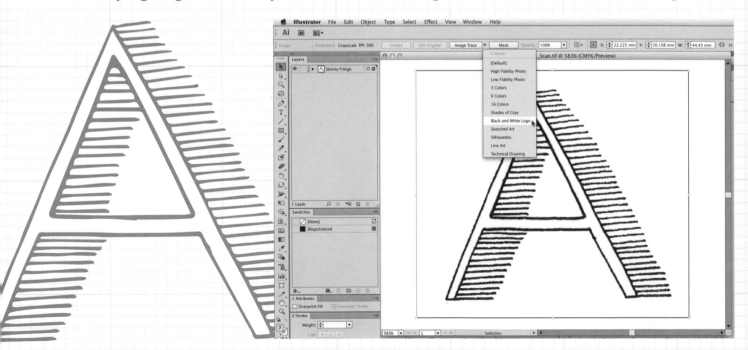

the best preset for this kind of work is probably Black and White Logo, while in CS5 or earlier there's a preset conveniently called Lettering which works pretty well. You could also take pot luck and click directly on the Image Trace button, but this will only guess which preset to use, so may not give the best results. Once you're happy with what you see, click the Expand button in the same Toolbar and hey presto – one vector character ready to go. If you're interested in exploring the custom settings for image tracing, you can access the dedicated panel at Window > Image Trace. *It's also worth mentioning that Illustrator CS6 has introduced some major improvements to the accuracy of this feature.*

Manual redrawing with Adobe Illustrator

The alternative is to redraw your character manually, something that you may prefer for simpler characters with less fine detail. The key to getting this right is mastery of the Pen tool. With a little practice it's actually quite easy to master, and adjusting what you've drawn is relatively simple too. If you choose to explore this method, start by importing your scan to a blank Illustrator document, and lock the layer once it's in position so you can't accidentally select it every time you click above it. Now all you have to do is carefully redraw the edges of your character, using the scan as a guide. The Pen tool works like

this: Click once, then click again without dragging the cursor, and you'll get angled corners at each anchor point joined by straight lines. If you want to create a curve off an anchor point, click at the next point you want to create on your path but drag without releasing the mouse button and the line will become a curve, complete with adjustment handles which you can use later for fine tuning. If you want to switch back to straight lines again, click once on the last anchor point you created, then continue drawing your path and you'll be back to angled corners and straight lines once again.

It won't take long for you to get the hang of this – it's all pretty intuitive – and you'll soon be able to make a swift decision about whether to trace or redraw your characters, depending on their complexity and level of detailing. You may even decide that a combination of both methods is the best way to go.

Left: Select the appropriate preset from the drop-down Toolbar menu and your scan will be auto-traced quickly and with a high degree of accuracy. This font is Skinny Fringe by Michelle Tilly (see page 44).

Right: Learning to redraw your characters manually with Illustrator's Pen tool is an intuitive process, and it won't take you long to get to grips with the techniques involved. This font is Control Chaos by Sarah Lu (see page 28).

DIGITIZING YOUR FONTS

The selection of software solutions that enable you to turn a set of individual glyphs into a usable digital font is not particularly extensive, but the options that are available do the job very well. Software choice should be governed largely by the level of sophistication your own font projects require. I've chosen one of the more 'entry level' applications to showcase here, TypeTool by FontLab.

FontLab (www.fontlab.com) bill TypeTool as their basic font editor, suitable for students and hobbyists as well as creative professionals, so it's a good choice for anyone new to the world of font creation. It runs on Macs and PCs, but do check compatibility with your particular system before you install any software to be sure you're fully compatible with the latest version.

The following pages will give you a short overview of what you can achieve; the software is accompanied by a 380-page manual which covers everything in detail, but don't let the length of this put you off as it's well written using easy-to-understand terms.

The Font window

When you begin to create a new font, something you can do either by clicking on File > New from the menu bar or by opening an existing digital font that you wish to edit, the first window you'll see is the main Font window (see below), containing all the available slots for each glyph. The font that appears in the screen shots here is Archive Tilt, as used for the main headings in this book.

THE TOOL PALETTE
The Tool palette features tools which will be broadly familiar to anyone that has used Adobe Illustrator, CorelDRAW and so on. There's an Edit Tool, an Eraser, a Knife, a Ruler, and a Pen Tool. There are also tools for adding different types of adjustment point, for basic shape creation, and for Rotating, Scaling, Slanting and Free Transforming.

You'll notice that some of the slots appear greyed out. This is because these slots haven't been assigned a glyph and are empty – white slots represent the range of glyphs that already exist in the font – and the characters that appear in grey slots are for reference only. Glyphs must be added to their pre-assigned slots in order to work correctly when typed using a standard keyboard. To edit an existing glyph, double click it in the Font window to reveal the Glyph window.

The Glyph window

The Glyph window (see above) is where all the drawing and/or editing takes place. If you click on a grey slot, this window will contain a rough representation of the assigned glyph, which you can hide by deselecting the background layer using View > Show Layers > Background.

The window contains a background grid and displays separate adjustable guides for cap height (the top edge of all upper case letters), baseline (the line upon which all the letters in a word sit), and the x-height (the top edge of the lower case letters). There are also adjustable guides to indicate the width of the glyph. These are just as important as they define the spacing that exists between each character when paired with another.

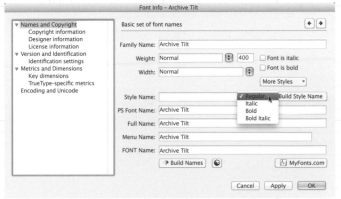

The Font Info panel

Before we discuss how to import your own font designs into TypeTool, we should talk about one more important panel. The Font Info panel is the place to enter all the information that describes your font. Without this information, the design software you plan to use in conjunction with your own hand-drawn font won't know how to list it in its font menu.

You'll see from our example above that the family name, Archive Tilt, is in place alongside information about the weight and the width, which is important if there's more than one font in the family with the same family name. If all the information is added to the upper part of this panel, clicking the 'Build Names' button will automatically fill the rest of the fields for you.

Importing outlines from Adobe Illustrator

It is, of course, possible to create outline fonts directly in the TypeTool Glyph panel, but I prefer to use Illustrator primarily because the working area is more flexible. It's also possible to work on more than one glyph side-by-side in Illustrator, which can flag up important design issues during the creative process. We've already talked about creating vector outlines in Illustrator on pages 150–51, but it's also important to note that you need to alter one of Illustrator's default preference settings to ensure this process works properly. From the Illustrator menu bar, go to Illustrator > Preferences > File Handling & Clipboard and check that the 'Clipboard on Quit' settings match the screen shot shown below. If it's set to copy as a PDF, the image you paste into TypeTool will be a grey bitmap rather than a vector outline.

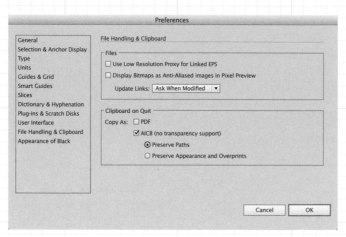

For the next stage of the process, it's important to make sure all the glyphs you've created in Illustrator are a consistent size before you paste them into the appropriate slot in TypeTool's Glyph panel. The default cap height in the Glyph panel is 700 points, so it makes sense to use this measurement as the standard for your Illustrator files as well. I'm going to use the 'A' from Skinny Fringe by Michelle Tilly that I auto-traced on page 150 for this exercise.

Create a new Illustrator document that is at least 700 points high. I recommend that you make your document 900 points high and at least 1200 points wide (to accommodate wider glyphs such as the 'M'), then place guides 100 points in from the top, bottom and left edges, giving you an accurate 700-point-high working area. Copy and paste your vector glyph into the document and align it with the top intersection of the guides as shown in the screen shot below. You'll notice that the 'A' is currently much less than 700 points in height, but this doesn't matter because vectors can be sized up infinitely with no loss in quality.

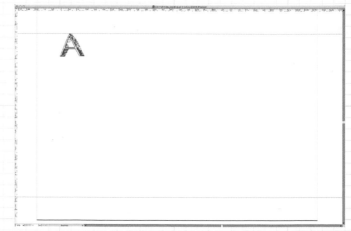

Select all the vector paths that make up the glyph and group them using Object > Group, then size everything up to 700 points in height. You can do this by clicking and dragging the lower-right corner of the grouped object to the right whilst holding down the shift key to maintain the object's proportions. Alternatively, you can enter the precise values in the relevant fields in the Application bar, making sure that you've checked the chain button next to the width field to once again maintain width-to-height proportions.

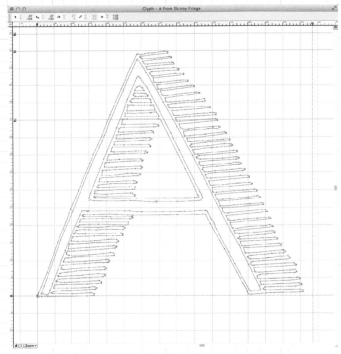

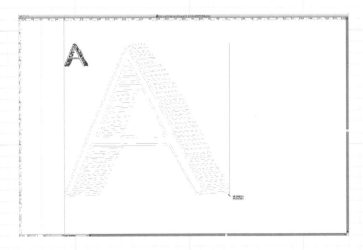

Once you're happy that your glyph is exactly the right size keep it selected and copy it, Cmd+c on a Mac or Ctrl+c on a PC, then switch to TypeTool. Open the main Font window if you haven't already done so and double click in the 'A' slot to open a new Glyph window. Paste the vector paths held on your clipboard with Cmd+v on a Mac or Ctrl+v on a PC, and the glyph will be pasted neatly into the window at the correct cap height and to the preset baseline (see above right). Now save your file, close the current Glyph window and you're ready to move on to the letter 'B'.

As this is simply a brief overview of the process, I would urge anyone to obtain some trial software so you can have a taster of what's to come before diving in. But using a software package like TypeTool is not as difficult as it may first appear, and it's the best way to make the most of the fonts that you've created on paper or in Illustrator.

• •

If you're hooked on digital font creation and want to raise the bar in terms of the sophistication of the software, take a look at FontLab Studio, which is used by all the major font foundries. As with TypeTool, details and downloads are available at www.fontlab.com.

THE ANATOMY OF A FONT

The hand-drawn fonts in this book are, by their very nature, unique. However, they still share features with every other typeface that's ever been designed, all of which are governed by the shape of the 26 standard letters (and the other glyphs) in a regular Roman character set. The diagram below highlights the principal features of a font.

This font is FTI-64 by Lee Suttey (see page 52).

GLOSSARY

Aperture: The gap formed when a counter isn't fully enclosed, for example in an 'a'.

Character: This usually refers to one particular letterform in a font which can be either a letter, a number, a punctuation mark, or a symbol such as an ampersand (&). In other words, 'A' and 'a' are the same *character* but different *glyphs* (see below).

Counter: The interior area within any glyph, counters can be either open or completely enclosed by strokes. For example, the upper part of a lowercase 'e' is a closed counter, whilst the lower part is an open counter.

Cursive: This term is used in connection with any font that is styled after handwriting.

Eye: Technically a counter, the 'eye' is specifically the enclosed space in the top half of a lowercase 'e'.

Font: A collection of glyphs at a specific size and weight. The term is also used to describe the digital files that are installed on your computer, and which allow you to use and print typefaces on your Mac or PC.

Glyph: The visual representation of a unique character within a font. For example, every font is likely to have at least a couple of glyphs for each letter – a lower case and an upper case. Some fonts will also contain alternative versions of characters, especially in the case of OpenType (see page 145) or handwriting fonts.

Lower case: The small letters of a typeface. The term originates from the days when metal type was composed by hand, and small letters were kept in the lower compartments of a type case.

Monospaced: A typeface in which all available glyphs occupy the same horizontal width in a line of text.

PostScript: In the typographic world, PostScript is the page description language created in the 1980s. It enables scalable fonts to be generated from a vector-based original at any size, and provides the means by which computers transmit complete pages to a PostScript-equipped printing device, such as a laser printer.

Proportional: A typeface in which all available glyphs occupy different horizontal widths in a line of text.

Sans serif: A typeface that doesn't feature serifs.

Serif: The little stroke that sometimes appears at the end of a heavier stroke. Serifs generally taper to a point in fonts that are classified as 'serif' typefaces.

Slab Serif: A serif that's rectangular rather than tapered, with a heavy blunt end.

Stroke: Any line used to construct a glyph, as in a 'pen stroke'.

Stroke contrast: The difference between the thick and thin strokes in any one glyph.

Typeface: A set of characters that share specific design characteristics (see page 144).

Upper case: The capital letters of a typeface. Capitals were kept in the upper compartments of a type case storing metal type for hand composition.

Weight: The description, based on the relative thickness of the strokes, of the various fonts within any one typeface.

Wayne Blades

Wayne has two decades' experience as a graphic designer, working for design companies and publishers across the southeast of England. He's currently Art Director at the Ivy Press (and couldn't resist contributing a couple of fonts to this book) and is renovating a 1930s property in Hastings in his spare time (which he wishes he'd never started).

Emma Frith

Emma studied at Loughborough University of Art & Design and graduated with a BA (Hons) degree in 1996. She sought a career in publishing in 2003, working as a craft coordinator for a book publisher. She continues to take on commissioned work alongside her day job – for wedding card designs, CD covers for local bands, photography and mixed media paintings to name a few.

Katie Greenwood

Katie can usually be found searching for and taking images in Brighton as well as farther afield. Her other loves of design, typography and illustration have led her to doodle away many a spare hour, and to blog about all things creative at www.katiegreenwood.com.

Vanessa Hamilton

Vanessa is a freelance graphic designer, illustrator, garden designer and avid knitter. She studied graphic design at Central Saint Martins, London, then worked full time in book publishing until she decided to branch out on her own to explore other areas of design. Vanessa now works from her home studio in the country, alternating between the drawing board and the computer screen.

Tonwen Jones

Tonwen studied graphic design and illustration at Central Saint Martins before completing her MA, and has been working as a freelance illustrator for the last nine years. She works mainly in collage, often referencing her large collection of 1950s magazines in which she searches for images, objects and textures to manipulate her surrealist creations, revealing her comical take on everyday life. Tonwen also likes to draw complex pattern motifs in ink or pen, mixing styles and techniques. Her clients include *The Guardian*, *Globe and Mail*, *TimeOut* and *Eurostar Magazine*. Check out Tonwen's work here: www.tonwenjones.co.uk

Sarah Lu

Born in 1980, Sarah Lu has been drawing, creating and crafting all her life. She grew up with classics such as Blue Peter and Morph on the TV, and in later years took to the digital movement like a 'duck to water'. She fell in love with typography at the age of 11 and by 21 she had graduated with a BA (Hons) in Graphic Design. To this day, Sarah still uses her practical 'handmade' and 'low-tech' skills as the basis of all her creative design work.

Dave Pentland

Graphic design has been Dave's passion from a very young age, and after leaving education he decided to go and intern and learn how the industry works. He began at Red Design in Brighton, England, and subsequently moved to Cannes in France, where he worked for a publishing company, before returning to Brighton.

Holly Sellors

Holly has been drawing since she could pick up a pencil. As a self-taught artist/illustrator, Holly has found it difficult to become known, but with determination and motivation it can be done. Holly takes inspiration from the world around her and is a keen photographer, constantly collecting images to reference as part of her work as well as keeping a sketchbook filled with notes and ideas. To see more of her art, visit www.projectlumino.co.uk.

Lee Suttey

Lee completed an Illustration degree at Portsmouth University, gaining a 1st Class BA (Hons). He then continued his education with a Graphic Design and Illustration MA. He has also taken part in a touring exhibition with his Artist Book work called *Changing Pages*, curated by the Collins Gallery. On leaving education, Lee worked for various multimedia and graphic design agencies in London before setting up on his own as a graphic designer for print and screen under the name Visual Function. Lee loves using his sketchbooks and drawing to generate ideas, and this is where his love of hand-drawn type originates.

Scott Suttey

Since gaining an Illustration degree, Scott has worked as a designer/illustrator in both freelance and full-time capacities. He's dealt with a wide variety of clients including publishers, government organizations and charities on projects for print and screen. He always has a sketchbook within reach and often uses hand-drawn type to complement his illustration work.

Michelle Tilly

Michelle studied illustration at UWE Bristol, and later graduated in 2006 with an MA in Sequential Illustration and Design. She's a smaller-than-average person who works with larger-than-life clients including *The Guardian*, Specsavers, *Q Magazine*, Vodafone, &&& Creative and The Ivy Group. She draws inspiration from the everyday and the odd, and enjoys creating characters based on the folks around her. Check out her work here: www.runningforcrayons.co.uk

Alex Wells

Alex is an artist, photographer and designer with a degree in Illustration. Alex has illustrated artwork for several successful bands and received an award for a *Puffin Post* cover design in 2011. She has contributed to two illustrated books, and is currently collaborating on several more books and illustration projects.

ACKNOWLEDGEMENTS

The first people I need to thank here are the nice folk at The Ivy Press because – time to admit it – this book wasn't my idea. There, I've said it and it's all out in the open now. The concept for this book was formed at The Ivy Press before they were kind enough to ask me to become involved in the project, so a big thank you to Sophie Collins, Wayne Blades, Jayne Ansell and Judith Chamberlain-Webber for inviting me on-board. Thanks also to Steve Luck for making sure my text made sense and wasn't full of embarrassing mistakes.

The team at Ivy also played a central role in the process of tracking down the talented designers and illustrators who provided the fonts which fill this book. Particular thanks to Wayne, Emma, Katie, Vanessa, Tonwen, Sarah, Dave, Holly, Lee, Scott, Michelle and Alex. I hope I've interpreted your concepts correctly.

Thanks also to Ted Harrison and Lisa Devlin at FontLab for their support and advice during the writing of the section on 'Digitizing Your Fonts'.

Finally, and as always, thanks to my wife Sarah for uncomplainingly allowing me to skip cooking the dinner on several occasions when it was my turn but I was running too close to a deadline. I shall do my best to make up the time.